SHAUN HILL'S
QUICK & EASY
VEGETABLE
C O O K E R Y

ABOUT THE AUTHOR

Master chef Shaun Hill has worked in some of Britain's top restaurants and hotels, including the Lygon Arms, the Gay Hussar and Blakes Hotel in London. For the past eight years he has been Chef and Director of Gidleigh Park in Devon, one of the country's finest country-house hotels. He regularly appears on television and in the national press, where the combination of his wit and charm and his considerable culinary talents have earned him a devoted following.

The experience he has gained has produced many accolades including, most recently, The Egon Ronay Cellnet Guide's most prestigious award, 1993's 'Chef of the Year'.

SHAUN HILL'S
QUICK & EASY
VEGETABLE
COOKERY

BBC BOOKS

Published by BBC Books, a division of
BBC Enterprises Limited, Woodlands,
80 Wood Lane, London W12 0TT

First published 1993
Copyright © Shaun Hill 1993

ISBN 0 563 36432 7

Designed by Peter Bridgewater
Photographs by James Murphy
Styling by Jane McLeish
Home Economist Simon Collins

Set in Bembo by BP Integraphics, Bath, Avon
Printed and bound in Great Britain by Clays Ltd, St Ives plc
Colour separations by Technik Ltd, Berkhamsted
Colour printing by Lawrence Allen Ltd, Weston-super-Mare
Cover printed by Clays Ltd, St Ives plc

CONTENTS

Introduction

Vegetables have a spot of problem with their image. Having to serve as a term of abuse for the slow-witted doesn't help. This book's purpose is to give some ideas on their use and how to make more fuss of them, given that you have not unlimited time, resources or money at your disposal. It is not necessarily a book for vegetarians, certainly not just for vegetarians anyway, and there is no intention of dressing up vegetables as some sort of meat substitute. Rather the objective is to make good use of the range and quality of fresh vegetables now available.

Despite big advances in the year-round supply of vegetables, this is a neglected area of cookery: an odd state of affairs considering the strong tradition in Britain of eating vegetables with every meal. Perhaps we have allowed the influences of America where the salads tend to predominate, and France where vegetables are less central to the meal, to affect our eating habits.

It is important to accept a few basic ideas. First, vegetables are not just 'veg', filler to surround a piece of meat or fish. They are becoming too expensive to perform the function of a nosebag of hay anyway so you may as well make the best of them. Secondly, there is such a magnificent diversity in texture, flavour and availability. Seasonal fluctuations will constantly alter the possibilities on offer. Importantly they will affect quality and price with the bonus of produce arriving at peak condition when the price is cheapest. In winter when you are fed up with brassica and celeriac you will have to buy imports. In summer and autumn when markets are full of prime produce, only a fool goes to the freezer counter.

Notes on the Recipes

- All recipes are for four persons unless the recipe says otherwise.
- Follow either the imperial or metric measures consistently when using a recipe. Don't mix the two.
- Use size 3 eggs throughout except where the recipe asks for large ones when you will need to use size 1.
- All spoon measurements are level spoons.
- All vegetables should be washed before use.
- Taste as you go along. When recipes call for, say, tomatoes it has been assumed that they are ripe. At different times of year they will sometimes have more, sometimes less, flavour so make adjustments accordingly.
- Similarly, Cheddar cheese means mature, preferably traditionally made, cheese. If you can't find any you may need to increase the quantities of mild Cheddar to compensate.

KITCHEN EQUIPMENT

The first essential is a sharp knife. Two or three of different sizes would be even better so long as they are also sharp. Keep your knives spotlessly clean and always wash them between cutting raw and cooked items.

A liquidiser is a genuine, labour-saving device. So too is a food processor. Anyone like myself who has spent hours in restaurant kitchens pushing sauces and soups through a sieve – or, worse, through muslin – in order to produce an inferior result will view these contraptions as godsent.

Some jobs which a food processor does well are still easier done by hand though, for they are a nuisance to clean and assemble. You must judge whether the time saved is worth the washing up created.

Nice but not essential is a wok or steamer. Woks are really versatile and I use my own for hot smoking and steaming as well as stir-frying.

A good range of saucepans which includes a heavy casserole for slow cooking or pot roasting is more use than any gadget. The right-sized pan saves time and money.

All other equipment is less important. I like home-made ice-cream, it is easy and inexpensive, so have indulged myself with a sorbet machine. If you have similar weaknesses, perhaps enjoy meringues and need an electric whisk or enjoy the speed of microwave cooking, this is also fine.

STORE-CUPBOARD INGREDIENTS

Each school of cooking – Indian, Chinese, Italian or whatever – demands a quite particular store-cupboard. A book of Chinese recipes will assume you have not just soy sauce but also black bean, hoisin and a spice range which includes star anise, ginger and five spice. There is little point in stocking up with such items unless you intend to use them periodically. On the other hand you will need a trolley full of such ingredients to begin even quite straight-forward recipes if you have no store-cupboard items at all.

I find the following to be an indispensable minimum. All else is, of course, a matter of taste and your own predilections where food is concerned. Remember that ground spices don't keep indefinitely so throw out and replace items like ground cinnamon or paprika if they have been open for weeks.

MUSTARD

Dijon mustard or powdered English, depending on whether you prefer the strong-tasting native variety or less powerful Dijon. My preference is for the latter. German and Swedish mustards are sweet and mild, good for children's food and those who prefer salad cream to mayonnaise.

Course or wholegrain mustards are generally well flavoured, with English varieties hotter than French. These are good but not versatile as ingredients.

OLIVE OIL

Olive oil comes in three main styles. Italian extra virgin oils are the most expensive and usually come in an elegantly crafted bottle with a designer label. They are powerful, concentrated oils and are best drizzled straight on to salads or whatever rather than used as an ingredient. They can be worth the money but should be used sparingly.

French olive oils are lighter and fruitier. They are also usually cheaper and make very good dressings.

Most Spanish or Greek olive oils tend to be rather greasy tasting and lack the aristocratic style of the other two. Olive oils which merely announce themselves as olive oil are usually rubbish, a throwback from the days when this was considered a medicinal product and stored on the shelf next to embrocations. You are better off spending your cash on a decent groundnut or vegetable oil at an equivalent price.

OTHER OILS

Light sesame oil and an all-purpose quality cooking oil such as groundnut.

TOMATO PASSATA

This is a comparatively recent product to arrive on supermarket shelves. It is made from sieved plum tomatoes and is the same strength as the fresh item not a concentrate. It is not expensive and usually will be sold in ½ litre (1 pint) jars or bottles so you don't get the tinny taste of canned tomato.

Tomato purée is a dreadful, bitter product. I recommend you use it only when there is no choice and even then with caution.

Fresh tomatoes are generally at their best in late summer. At other times, most varieties are underflavoured and unsuited for use in cooking. Best kept for salads. Recipe books by grand French or Italian cooks which call for tomato will understand it to be a strong, sun-ripened Mediterranean sort rather than our own more delicate types. My advice is to add some passata to such recipes in order to bridge the difference.

CHEESE

Cheddar cheese is one of the world's great ingredients. The essential word to look for when shopping for it is 'mature'. 'Farmhouse' doesn't mean much, least of all a connection with quaint agricultural buildings.

Pecorino or Parmesan. Pecorino is a firm, dry sheep's-milk cheese which gives a more subtle taste than Parmesan and is well worth searching out. Parmesan should be easier to find and is quick to grate from a small block. The ready-grated stuff in small drums is only OK.

COMMERCIAL SAUCES

For Worcestershire sauce, use Lea & Perrins. For soy sauce, look for a brewed product, Japanese brands are usually best. For chilli sauce, I prefer Tabasco partly because I'm accustomed to its strength and so find it easy to use. There are several good chilli sauces on the market however.

HERBS AND SPICES

I keep nutmeg and black peppercorns. Cinnamon is useful and as it is used often rarely has the chance to get old. For other spices, buy the smallest amount possible of any spice you need, as you need it.

Dried herbs are a mystery. It is almost impossible to tell one from another with your eyes shut as they all taste like stale old tea-leaves. Those that are distinctive like thyme don't taste anything like the fresh item. If fresh herbs aren't available buy freeze-dried herbs which at least retain their colour.

VINEGAR

White wine vinegar is a staple item. Other varieties will be specific to certain dishes or styles of cooking. Of course you can buy them if you intend actually to use them.

Sherry vinegar has a rich oak taste and plenty of sherry aroma. It is good for certain dressings and to liven up stews.

Balsamic vinegar from Modena is an almost sweet vinegar. It is made on the solera system like sherry and aged in a procession of barrels, each one made from some different aromatic wood like juniper. Real Balsamic vinegar is aged for long periods, thirty years is not rare, and has an almost syrup-like consistency. It is also expensive. Serviceable imitations are now available in most supermarkets. In northern Italy it is used on fresh strawberries as well as salads.

Raspberry vinegar is refreshing as a change but not versatile in the way of ordinary wine vinegar. Malt vinegar is made from beer and has its supporters. I am not really one of them although it has quite a nostalgic taste with chips for persons of my age.

Non-brewed condiment is what it sounds like, inferior.

BREADCRUMBS

If you need to make breadcrumbs, do so by cutting white bread – not too fresh – into cubes and processing it in a blender or a food processor. The paddle attachment of a mixer at low speed would also do the trick.

COOKING VEGETABLES

For years most vegetables, especially root vegetables like carrots, were cooked until virtual sludge. The arrival of 'Nouvelle Cuisine' in the 1970s brought a reaction against such maltreatments and quite suddenly it became *de rigueur* amongst smart people to leave vegetables crisp. As with most cookery trends this period proved a mixed blessing and silly persons took the idea to absurd lengths. In no time disconsolate diners could be seen pursuing rock-hard lumps of cauliflower and concrete beans across their plates.

So what is correct? Neither, of course. Basically you should cook any food in the way you would personally enjoy eating it and be guided by your own tastebuds rather than any perception of what's clever or expected. My own preference tends towards cooking root vegetables such as carrots until they are quite tender, soft enough to be pierced with a sharp knife and offer little resistance, but to cook green vegetables such as courgettes, french beans, or mange-tout peas so that they are still quite crunchy.

I have heard people say that one shouldn't boil vegetables in too much water, the theory being that all the goodness will be leached away. I have never found this and on the contrary find that when green vegetables are dropped into plenty of boiling water the water will reboil very quickly, keeping all the freshness and colour of the vegetables. Two final points on boiling. If possible use a lidded pan, or your kitchen will resemble a steam bath. Secondly, remember the salt. Your cooking liquor doesn't have to be like the Dead Sea but it must have some salt to bring out the flavour of your vegetables. Dried pulses like chick peas or lentils are an exception. They are being rehydrated as well as cooked and should be seasoned afterwards.

Roasting and grilling can be very successful methods of cooking vegetables but are not as versatile. Only tender vegetables are suitable for grilling and large items such as onions or aubergine for roasting. As far as possible use the cooking method most sympathetic to the produce. Tender young carrots will make superb crudités, larger, old carrots may be better suited to being chopped for carrot timbale or making into soup, as they may well have more flavour. Try to keep your options open until after you have done the shopping.

STARTERS, SAVOURIES AND SNACKS

Defining starters in a meal which consists largely of vegetable and fruit dishes is partly a matter of size and partly a matter of taste. A smaller dish can take proportionately more spicing and therefore be more suitable. Otherwise a salad will fit the bill admirably.

Most people eat only one 'proper' meal a day and will munch a snack of something either sweet or comforting to keep up body sugar levels and prevent any stomach rumbling in between. Hot sandwiches (page 29) or potato cakes (page 23) are ideal for such moments. Certainly some savoury morsel is essential for those of us prone to the temptation of a lunchtime drink but who still need to keep alert for the afternoon's work.

CONTENTS

MASHED POTATO CAKES WITH OLIVES AND CAPERS

SERVES
— 4 —

This would make an acceptable breakfast with maybe a poached egg or some tomato sauce.

Wash, peel and boil the potatoes until cooked.

Drain off the water and mash the potatoes. Do not beat or whisk them. Roughly chop the olives and capers. Add these and the olive oil, salt and pepper to the mash and stir them in.

Shape into eight 1 cm (½ inch) thick patties. They should look like hamburgers or fish cakes.

Dip the potato cakes in the egg and sprinkle with breadcrumbs.

Shallow fry until golden brown, around 5 minutes on each side.

INGREDIENTS

450 g (1 lb) maincrop potatoes
30 pitted green olives
20 capers
2 tablespoons olive oil
Salt and freshly ground black pepper
1 egg, beaten
100 g (4 oz) fresh breadcrumbs (see page 17)
Vegetable oil for frying

*I*TALIAN VEGETABLE ANTIPASTO

S E R V E S

— 4 —

8 young sweet carrots, peeled

1 red or green pepper, de-seeded

2 medium courgettes, trimmed

1 clove garlic, crushed

Olive oil for frying

1 tablespoon clear honey

4 tablespoons tomato passata (see page 16)

1 tablespoon Dijon mustard

1 teaspoon lemon juice

1 teaspoon powdered ginger

100g (4 oz) button mushrooms

1 small jar green pitted olives

The choice of vegetables is largely up to you. Root vegetables aren't particularly suitable, otherwise anything which gives a contrast of colour and flavour is good. Cauliflower florets, french beans, pickling onions or aubergine would all be great instead of or as well as my selection.

Cut the carrots, pepper and courgettes into roughly equal sized pieces of around 1 cm (½ inch).

Fry the garlic in a few drops of oil. Add the honey, tomato, mustard, lemon juice and ginger and stir well.

In a separate frying-pan fry the carrots, mushrooms, courgettes and pepper in turn for 3 minutes each. Add to the sauce then bring this to the boil and simmer for 2 or 3 minutes. Add the olives.

Allow to cool. The vegetables should still be crunchy. Serve cold.

SWEDE AND CHEDDAR SOUFFLÉ

SERVES

—— 4 ——

Perhaps this is not everyone's idea of a quick dish. With only a little care, though, it is not difficult and the swedes may be prepared and cooked in advance so long as you remember to keep the cooking water or else substitute it with milk.

―――――――

Preheat the oven to Gas Mark 6, 200°C (400°F).

Butter or oil a 1 litre (2 pint) soufflé dish. Butter or oil a double folded strip of silver foil long enough and wide enough to fit around the dish and rise 5 cm (2 inches) above the rim as a collar. If the foil isn't stiff an elastic band may help to keep it in place.

Boil the swede in a lidded saucepan until tender, around 25 minutes. When cooked, drain the cooking water into a bowl or jug and keep it for later.

Wipe the saucepan clean then melt the butter over a low heat. Stir in the flour and cook gently for 1 minute. Measure out 350 ml (12 fl oz) of the cooking water and pour this, a third at a time, on to the flour and butter mixture. Stir until the sauce reboils each time.

Mash the swede and season with salt and pepper. This can be done by hand but is easier in a food processor. You can also do the next stage in it.

Add the sauce which you have made using the cooking liquid, together with all 6 egg yolks. Mix well.

Whisk the egg whites with ¼ teaspoon of salt and the cream of tartar until stiff.

Turn the swede mixture into a bowl. Stir in a quarter of the whisked egg white. This will make the mixture slacker and easier to handle. Then fold in the remaining whisked egg white and the Cheddar cheese.

Spoon the mixture into the prepared soufflé dish and bake it in the middle of the oven for 45 minutes until golden brown and puffed up. Serve immediately.

INGREDIENTS

450 g (1 lb) swede, peeled and cut into approximately 1 cm (½ inch) pieces
50 g (2 oz) unsalted butter
40 g (1½ oz) plain flour
Salt and freshly ground black pepper
6 large eggs, separated
¼ teaspoon cream of tartar
175 g (6 oz) mature Cheddar cheese, grated

TEMPURA

(DEEP-FRIED VEGETABLES WITH GINGER AND SOY DIP)

SERVES

—— 4 ——

FOR THE BATTER

250 ml (8 fl oz) water, as cold as you can get it
1 egg
100 g (4 oz) plain flour
50 g (2 oz) cornflour
A pinch of salt

VEGETABLES

2 red peppers, halved and de-seeded
2 courgettes, trimmed
1 aubergine, trimmed
1 bunch spring onions, topped and tailed
Oil for frying

FOR THE DIP

Small knob of fresh ginger
Soy sauce
Chilli sauce

If you can buy tempura batter mix in an oriental delicatessen so much the better. This is what happens in all the Japanese restaurants I know. Alternatively this batter recipe is simple and works well.

As the vegetables are fried from raw and not parboiled, the thickness of the slices into which they are cut is important. Too thick and they will never cook, too thin and you will taste only the frying batter not the strip of vegetable inside.

Make the batter by whisking together the cold water, egg, flour, cornflour and salt.

Cut the peppers into 5 mm (¼ inch) strips.

Cut the courgettes and aubergine as if you were making them into potato chips.

Dip the vegetables into tempura batter and deep-fry. Don't have the oil smoking hot or the batter will brown before the vegetable is properly cooked. If you have a cooking thermometer, 190°C (370°F) is a good temperature. Cook the vegetables in batches rather than overload the fryer. The results should be light, crisp and crunchy, there should be no greasiness.

Make an accompanying dip by peeling and chopping the small knob of ginger and combining it with Japanese soy sauce and a few drops of chilli or Tabasco sauce.

GRILLED RADICCHIO AND SWISS CHEESE TOASTS

SERVES
— 4 —

This is a version of the Swiss dish, Raclette. Raclette cheese is sliced very thinly and then layered on toast and grilled. It smells horrible as it cooks but tastes delicious. For this dish a more accessible cheese like Gruyère or Emmental can be used.

Boil the potatoes in salted water until tender. Drain and allow to cool. Cut into slices.

Whisk the olive oil, lemon juice, salt and pepper together to make a dressing. Toss the radicchio leaves and potatoes in it.

Toast the bread lightly on each side. Place the slices on a baking tray and divide the radicchio and potato salad equally on to each slice.

Cover each slice of bread with four slices of Swiss cheese and place under a hot grill until the cheese is completely melted, about 2 minutes.

Serve immediately with chutney or pickle.

INGREDIENTS

4 new potatoes, scrubbed
2 tablespoons olive oil
Juice of 1 lemon
Salt and pepper
2 small heads radicchio
4 slices good white bread
16 thin slices Swiss cheese
  (about 450 g or 1 lb)
Chutney or pickle, to serve
  (optional)

ROAST PEPPERS WITH HERBS, LEMON AND OLIVE OIL

SERVES

— 4 —

INGREDIENTS

8 red peppers
8 yellow peppers
Small bunch of fresh
    marjoram, oregano or
    thyme
16 black olives
Salt and pepper
Zest and juice of 2 lemons
A little groundnut oil for
    frying
150 ml (5 fl oz) extra
    virgin olive oil
Crusty bread, to serve

If you have difficulty in peeling roast or grilled peppers, try wrapping them in food wrap or foil as they cool down after roasting. The skins will then slip off easily.

Roast the peppers in a moderate oven (Gas Mark 4, 180°C or 350°F) or grill them for 5 minutes so that the skin blisters but the vegetable doesn't burn. Turn them frequently. About 10 minutes in all should do the job. Allow to cool.

Cut the peppers in half lengthwise and scrape out the seeds and any pith. Peel them – the skin should scrape off without any trouble.

Lay the peppers on cold plates. Pick some herbs and scatter these and the olives around the plates. Season with salt and pepper.

Peel the zest from the lemons. Cut away any pith and slice the zest into thin strips. Use a zester if you have one. Squeeze the juice into a small bowl and add the zest to it.

Heat enough groundnut oil in a frying-pan to deep-fry the zest. When the oil is hot lift out the zest from the juice, pat it dry on kitchen paper and deep-fry it. This should take only a few seconds. To take the zest out of the oil, I find it easiest to have another pan or fireproof container standing by and a strainer, then pour the hot oil and zest into that so the strainer catches all the fried zest.

Scatter the fried zest over each plate. Finish the dish by pouring a tablespoon of olive oil over each plate followed by a few drops of the lemon juice. Serve with plenty of warm crusty bread.

HOT MUSHROOM, CARAMELISED ONION AND CHEESE SANDWICH

SERVES

— 4 —

M ore lunch than snack.

———

Fry the onion in a little oil. When the onion starts to cook, losing volume and gaining colour, add the sugar. Stir well and cook for 2 minutes. Add the vinegar and let this cook for a further 2 minutes.

Add the mushrooms and fry until cooked. Drain off any liquid and add a few leaves of thyme.

Grill the bread on one side. Turn over the bread and sprinkle the cheese on the untoasted side. Return the bread to the grill until the cheese melts.

Fill the sandwiches with caramelised onion and mushrooms and serve straightaway.

INGREDIENTS

*1 large onion, peeled and
   sliced
A little oil for frying
1 teaspoon sugar
1 teaspoon wine vinegar
100 g (4 oz) mushrooms,
   sliced
1 sprig of fresh thyme
8 slices white bread
100 g (4 oz) mature
   Cheddar cheese, grated*

SWEETCORN PANCAKES WITH BAKED TOMATO

SERVES
— 4 —

1 large egg
300 ml (10 fl oz) milk
50 g (2 oz) plain flour
2 tablespoons melted butter
  or vegetable oil
Salt and pepper
225 g (8 oz) sweetcorn
  kernels
4 tomatoes, halved
1 teaspoon olive oil
1 teaspoon wine vinegar

Sweetcorn is one of the few ingredients better tinned than frozen. Of course, fresh isn't bad either but fresh corn is only sold on the cob and really that's how it's best eaten.

Preheat the oven to Gas Mark 6, 200°C (400°F).

Make a batter by whisking together the egg, milk, flour, and half the butter or oil. Season.

If the corn is fresh or frozen drop it into boiling salted water for 5 minutes to cook. If it is tinned, you will just need to drain it.

Coarsely chop the corn kernels and add to the pancake batter.

Place tomatoes on a baking dish. Drizzle with the olive oil and vinegar. Season with salt and pepper. Bake in the oven until soft, about 10 minutes.

Use the remaining butter or oil for frying the pancakes. You want small pancakes for this dish so drop a tablespoonful of batter at a time into the pan leaving room between each pancake. Frying for 2 or 3 minutes on each side will cook them through and give a pleasing golden colour. Stack the cooked pancakes on a hot dish in a warm place until you have used up all the batter.

Serve hot, accompanied by the tomatoes.

GRILLED BABY VEGETABLES

SERVES
—— 4 ——

As the vegetables for this dish are grilled from raw, tender specimens such as baby bunched carrots or new season leeks are ideal. The vegetables given here are just a guideline. Buy whatever is in peak condition and not monstrously expensive. You will find this method of cooking concentrates the flavour of the vegetables while keeping the texture crunchy like crudités.

INGREDIENTS

12 small carrots
12 young leeks
12 asparagus spears
12 baby sweetcorn
A little oil

Wash the vegetables and pat them dry with kitchen paper. Peel the carrots and trim off any tough-looking green parts of the leek. The asparagus shouldn't need peeling if it is recently harvested and in season but it is always worth checking the base of the stalks in case there are any spots of mould.

Brush the vegetables with oil. If you don't want to use a brush, turn the vegetables on a plate with oil. The aim is to give them a very light coating, just enough to prevent them sticking.

Grill the vegetables under a moderately hot grill in the order of how much cooking time they need. This selection would start with the carrots, followed by the leeks, then the asparagus and finally the sweetcorn. One or two leaves of the leeks may blacken too much during cooking. Just peel them off before serving.

BRUSCHETTA WITH TOMATO, CELERY AND CHIVES

SERVES

— 6 —

6 slices white 'country'
  bread (a pain de
  campagne *type of bread*
  is fine, factory-sliced
  bread is not)
1 clove of garlic
Extra virgin olive oil
6 ripe plum or beefsteak
  tomatoes
6 sticks of celery (about
  half an average sized
  celery)
1 bunch of chives
Salt and pepper
6 olives
50 g (2 oz) fresh Pecorino
  or Parmesan cheese

Dried, toasted and fried country breads in the Italian style such as bruschetta and crostini have caught the imagination in recent years. They perform the same function as their grander cousins, classical cuisine's canapés, and provide robust-tasting snacks to go with drinks or maybe a light first course.

The bread is a vehicle for whatever topping you fancy, much in the same way as a pizza base. Generally speaking this is not the moment for restrained or subtle flavours.

Toast the bread on both sides. Rub with the garlic clove and sprinkle with olive oil. Keep the garlic clove for later.

Peel and de-seed the tomatoes then cut them into dice. Plum tomatoes are easily peeled with a sharp knife. Beefsteak tomatoes will need dunking into boiling water for 10 seconds before peeling.

Wash the celery then peel it with a potato peeler. Cut into thin slices.

Chop the chives with a sharp knife or use scissors. Chives bruise easily.

Crush the clove of garlic with a little salt and the flat side of a knife. Mix together with 2 tablespoons of extra virgin olive oil, the tomatoes and celery. Season with a little more salt and plenty of milled black pepper.

Spoon this mixture on to the bruschetta and finish each slice with an olive and some shavings of Pecorino or Parmesan cheese.

ROAST PEPPERS WITH HERBS, LEMON AND OLIVE OIL (*page 28*)

POTATO GALETTES WITH SPINACH AND NUTMEG SAUCE

SERVES

— 4 —

The spinach and nutmeg is doing duty as sauce rather than just accompaniment so will need to be more robustly spiced and seasoned than might seem initially appropriate.

The crème fraîche or soured cream is there to provide some sharpness, a balance for the fried potato galette. If you don't normally use this type of cream and are not about to start, you can make a creditable substitute by acidulating a little double or whipping cream with a few drops of lemon juice or wine vinegar.

INGREDIENTS

225 g (8 oz) spinach
1 tablespoon soured cream
* or crème fraîche*
½ teaspoon nutmeg
Salt and pepper
2 large maincrop potatoes,
* peeled*
Vegetable oil for frying

Boil the spinach briefly in salted water than drain. It doesn't matter if there is some moisture left on the spinach leaves as you are going to purée them.

Put the spinach, soured cream, nutmeg and some salt and pepper into a liquidiser or a food processor and blend. Keep the sauce warm while you make the galettes.

To make the galettes coarsely grate the potatoes, adding a good pinch of salt, then compress them briefly, a dessertspoonful at a time. Heat a little oil in a frying-pan and cook the galettes until crisp on each side. This should take about 5 minutes in total.

Spoon the sauce on to warmed plates and place the potato galettes on top.

GRILLED BABY VEGETABLES (*page 31*)

CARROT AND SPRING ONION FRITTERS

SERVES

—— 4 ——

INGREDIENTS

50 g (2 oz) carrot, coarsely
grated
40 g (1½ oz) spring onion,
sliced
1 large egg, beaten
2 tablespoons breadcrumbs
(see page 17)
Vegetable oil for deep
frying

The quantity of spring onion may seem a little daunt-ing for those not thrilled by the prospect of onion breath. Don't be intimidated, the cooking process works wonders. This batch makes eight fritters. Double the quantity if you need more substantial portions.

Put the carrot, spring onion, egg and breadcrumbs into a bowl and combine. If the mixture does not look promis-ing at this stage don't lose heart, all will be well.

Heat oil to a depth of 2.5 cm (1 inch) in a frying-pan. Don't start frying until the oil is hot.

Drop the mixture into the oil a tablespoon at a time. You may need to cook the fritters in batches depending on how wide your pan is. The fritters cook in around 2 minutes.

Lift the fritters on to kitchen paper to drain for a few seconds then serve.

PARSNIP
AND LEEK CAKES

SERVES

— 4 —

The sweetness of parsnips and the astringency of members of the onion family like leeks marry well together. At the time of year when parsnips are at their best leeks will tend to be large and a bit coarse – just right for hash or treatments like this.

Peel the parsnips and cut them into evenly sized pieces. Boil or steam them until tender then drain well and mash.

Thinly slice the leeks (see page 83) and stew them gently in a little oil. When they have softened and are starting to colour add the curry powder. Cook for 1 minute then mix with the parsnip purée. Add salt and pepper to taste.

Add the breadcrumbs and egg. Mix thoroughly.

Form into 8 fishcake-like shapes and shallow-fry until golden brown on each side, about 8–10 minutes in all.

INGREDIENTS

450 g (1 lb) parsnips
225 g (8 oz) leeks
Groundnut oil
1 teaspoon curry powder
Salt and pepper
50 g (2 oz) breadcrumbs
  (see page 17)
1 egg, beaten

CARROT TIMBALE

SERVES

—— 4 ——

INGREDIENTS

450 g (1 lb) carrots, peeled
   and finely chopped or
   grated
1 small onion, peeled and
   finely chopped
25 g (1 oz) butter
Salt, pepper and white
   sugar
175 ml (6 fl oz) water
2 eggs, beaten
3 tablespoons Gruyère
   cheese, grated
1 tablespoon chopped fresh
   parsley

SAUCE

1 clove garlic, chopped
65 g (2½ oz) butter
450 g (1 lb) ripe tomatoes,
   quartered
50 g (2 oz) tomato passata
   or 25 g (1 oz) purée
100 ml (3½ fl oz) water
Salt and pepper

Preheat the oven to Gas Mark 6, 200°C (400°F).

Cook the carrots and onions in a saucepan with the butter until tender, about 5 minutes. Add a scant teaspoon of salt, a pinch of sugar and pepper.

Add the water and simmer over a low heat until all the liquid has evaporated. Allow to cool.

Add the eggs, cheese and parsley to the carrot and onion mixture and stir well.

Butter 4 ramekin dishes and fill these with the mixture. Cover with foil or food wrap and place in a roasting pan, one-third filled with hot water.

Bake in the oven for 30 minutes. Meanwhile make the sauce.

SAUCE

Sweat the garlic in the butter until transparent.

Add the tomatoes and tomato passata or purée.

Pour on the water, stir and cook gently for 15 minutes.

Season with salt and pepper then either sieve or liquidise the sauce.

Unmould the carrot timbales on to individual plates and spoon the sauce around them to serve.

CAULIFLOWER BEIGNETS

S E R V E S

—— 4 ——

Soft vegetables are good when deep-fried. There is a contrast of texture between soft interior and crisp shell. Be careful using them as side dishes though for they will get soggy if sharing a plate with anything wet such as stews or gravy. Chips are hard enough to withstand the competition but courgettes and boiled cauliflower aren't.

Try serving them with some relish or pickle, preferably something a little sharp. Alternatively put them in a salad with lemon dressing.

Divide the cauliflower into florets and boil in salted water until cooked. Don't overcook the cauliflower, around 10 minutes should be enough. Drain and leave to cool.

Make the batter by whisking together the egg yolk, olive oil, lager and flour. Season with salt and then in a separate bowl whisk the egg white until stiff. Fold the egg white into the batter.

Season the cauliflower florets with salt, pepper and nutmeg and dip them in the batter.

Deep-fry until golden brown, around 4–5 minutes, then drain on kitchen paper before serving.

INGREDIENTS

1 large cauliflower
1 egg, separated
2 tablespoons olive oil
150 ml (5 fl oz) lager
150 g (5 oz) plain flour
Salt, pepper and nutmeg
Oil for frying

SOUPS

Home-made soups need either a liquidiser or plenty of time. I have opted for the former. The centrifugal effect means you can thicken the soup by emulsion as well as by the blending of solid ingredients. A little olive oil or butter will thicken soup or sauce nicely. The real problem is what to do about stock.

If you intend making vegetable stock do so by heating a tablespoon of vegetable oil in a saucepan and gently sweating a sliced onion, leek, piece of celery and aubergine. Season with salt and pepper and add 1 litre (2 pints) of water. Let this come to the boil and simmer for 20 minutes. If you do not need to use it immediately, decant into a jug and refrigerate or freeze.

Realistically, very few people have home-made stock in their freezer and the bouillon cube manufacturers have yet to make a passable substitute – though my information is that they are working hard on it at the moment and are all too well aware of the limitations of the present rather salty product.

Most soups don't need stock but if you feel a soup will be too bland without a little help or aren't confident of the integral flavour of your ingredients then at least make up the stock carefully. Bring the cube and measured quantity of water (follow whatever it says on the packet) to the boil. Stir until the cube is completely dissolved and then simmer for a couple of minutes. That way you won't find unmixed and unexpected concentrations of the product in your soup. As you boil the stock you can add any suitable vegetable trimmings. Every little bit helps and will also take away any chemical taste from the powder or cube.

Always make up bouillon separately. Crumbling it straight into a soup or sauce is not good practice, and leads to the problems just mentioned.

CONTENTS

CHILLED CARROT SOUP WITH INDIAN SPICES

S E R V E S
— 4 —

Cold soup – indeed cold anything – needs to be more powerfully seasoned than warm or hot ones. If you have a scientific disposition, you can try this experiment: eat a spoonful of your favourite ice-cream, notice how refreshing it tastes, then warm up another mouthful and taste again – sickly sweet.

Similarly, cold soups need to be adjusted for their spicing and salt levels at the temperature they will be served. Indian spices suit this treatment rather well and even those of you not fond of curry should at least try a spoonful. There could be a pleasant surprise.

Use a heavy saucepan as you are going to stew the vegetables before you add the water. Cook the carrots and onion gently in the vegetable oil, covered, stirring occasionally. When the onion is soft stir in the spices and let them cook for 1 minute.

Add the water or vegetable stock and bring to the boil. Simmer for 15 minutes or until the carrots are very tender.

Purée the soup in a blender. You will need to do this in two or three batches.

Cool completely then chill until cold. Test for seasoning when the soup is cold as the salt content needed is different for hot and cold dishes. If the carrots were particularly sweet add a few drops of lemon juice. Garnish with the chives or spring onion.

INGREDIENTS

4 carrots, peeled and sliced
1 onion, peeled and sliced
1 tablespoon vegetable oil
*½ teaspoon ground
  coriander seeds, ½
  teaspoon jeera (ground
  roast cumin), ½ teaspoon
  ground ginger; or 1½
  teaspoons curry powder*
*600 ml (1 pint) water or
  vegetable stock*
Salt and pepper
Lemon juice
*Some chives or spring
  onion, chopped, for
  garnish*

CARDAMOM AND SPLIT PEA SOUP

S E R V E S
—— 4 ——

INGREDIENTS

200 g (7 oz) dried split peas
600 ml (1 pint) water
2 onions, peeled and chopped
2 cloves garlic, peeled and chopped
4 tablespoons olive oil
1 teaspoon ground cardamom
¼ teaspoon cayenne pepper
½ teaspoon ground cinnamon
600 ml (1 pint) vegetable stock or water
A bunch of parsley, chopped
Juice of ½ lemon
Salt and pepper

All pulses need either prolonged soaking or cooking. If you remember to do this in advance, dishes such as this are both quick and simple to make. I'm sure none of us know anyone silly enough to stand watching beans soak or split peas boil. And if we do, we are far too polite to say so.

Rinse the split peas then put them in a saucepan with 600 ml (1 pint) of water. Bring to the boil then reduce the heat, cover and simmer for 45 minutes.

Meanwhile fry the onion and garlic gently in olive oil until soft.

Mix in the spices and continue to fry gently for 5 minutes.

When the split peas are cooked, the spiced onion and garlic should be added to them along with the vegetable stock or water.

Add almost a tablespoon of chopped parsley per person. Add the lemon juice and stir well. Check the seasoning and add salt and pepper to taste.

POTATO AND TOMATO SOUP WITH BASIL SIPPETS

S E R V E S
—— 4 ——

This is a summer soup best made with new potatoes and seasonal ripe tomatoes. Fresh basil is absurdly expensive in winter anyway and the dried variety tastes like stale tea-leaves with no aroma.

———

Preheat the oven to Gas Mark 4, 180°C (350°F).

Melt the butter and gently stew the leeks for 5 minutes. Add 300 ml (½ pint) water and bring to the boil.

Add the new potatoes along with a good pinch of salt and reboil.

Add the remaining water. Reboil then simmer until the potato starts to disintegrate, about 15 minutes. If you have cut the potatoes quite small this shouldn't take long.

While the potatoes cook prepare the sippets (see below) and the tomatoes.

To prepare the tomatoes heat 1 tablespoon olive oil in a frying-pan and add the tomatoes. Let them cook on a moderate heat for a few minutes until they lose texture and take on the appearance of a thick sauce. Season with black pepper and salt.

Combine the tomatoes and potatoes plus their cooking liquid in a food processor for a few seconds. If you need to adjust the seasoning do so now. Serve hot with sippets on top.

Sippets are dried slices of bread. They give texture to a soup or stew in the same way as croutons. Make the sippets by thinly slicing the French bread (the ficelle variety is even better for this than baguette if you have a choice). Place the slices on a baking tray and bake them in the oven for 10 minutes to dry. Blend 1 tablespoon olive oil, the lemon juice and the basil in a liquidiser and spread over the sippets. Return them to the oven for 1 minute to heat through before placing on the soup.

INGREDIENTS

25 g (1 oz) butter
4 new season leeks, sliced
  (see page 83)
900 ml (1½ pints) water
450 g (1 lb) new potatoes,
  scrubbed and cut into
  pieces
Salt and black pepper
2 tablespoons olive oil
450 g (1 lb) tomatoes, cut
  into pieces
½ stick of French bread
Juice of ½ lemon
1 large bunch of basil

WATERCRESS AND POTATO SOUP

SERVES

—— 4 ——

INGREDIENTS

275 g (10 oz) watercress,
  well washed
75 g (3 oz) butter
1 medium onion, peeled
  and chopped
225 g (8 oz) potatoes,
  peeled
600 ml (1 pint) water
Salt and pepper
450 ml (15 fl oz) milk
2 egg yolks
150 ml (5 fl oz) double
  cream

Until recently, watercress's main role was as half the standard garnish for any steak or mixed grill in restaurants, the other half being a grilled tomato. The potential for this peppery, almost bitter plant is more exciting. Watercress soup has a clean springlike taste with body and texture provided by the potato.

Take care when buying watercress. Once the bottom leaves of a bunch start to yellow the watercress is fit only for the bin. It is in any case a mistake to use soups purely as a vehicle for leftovers or vegetables past their prime, the waste disposal unit is designed for this job.

Pick out about a fifth of the best watercress leaves. Chop them and keep to one side as garnish.

Melt the butter in a saucepan. Add the onion and let it cook gently for a minute while you cut the potato into dice. The size of the dice is not crucial, however the larger the potato pieces the longer they will take to cook. Add the potato pieces to the pan.

Roughly chop the watercress and add this also. Let it cook gently, without taking on colour, for 5 minutes.

Add the water and season with salt and pepper. Bring to the boil and simmer until the potato is cooked, around 15 minutes.

Add the milk then liquidise the soup in batches in a blender. If the soup has become too thick add extra milk.

Return the soup to the saucepan and bring it back to the boil. Meanwhile whisk together the egg yolks, cream and the watercress reserved for garnish. Remove the soup from the heat and stir in this mixture. Check the seasoning and serve.

If you don't intend serving the soup straightaway leave the last steps (the addition of the egg and cream) until you are ready to eat. The egg yolks will tend to curdle if subjected to prolonged boiling or careless reheating.

KESAKEITTO

(FINNISH SUMMER SOUP)

S E R V E S

— 4 —

In Finland this light summer soup is very popular. It's a real celebration of the season and will not taste nearly as good if frozen or even imported ingredients are used. The soup is a vehicle for the flavours in the fresh produce. The dill and parsley should provide lift and contrast but not dominate.

———

Add the salt to the water, bring to the boil and add the potatoes, carrots and cauliflower. Reboil and cook for 5 minutes.

Add the peas and spinach and cook for 5 minutes.

Whisk the flour and milk together then add it to the pot and stir well.

Bring to the boil and boil gently for 2–3 minutes to lessen the floury taste. Then add the dill and parsley to serve.

1 teaspoon salt
600 ml (1 pint) water
100 g (4 oz) small new potatoes, scrubbed and cut into 2.5 cm (1 inch) pieces
4 small carrots, peeled and cut into 2.5 cm (1 inch) pieces
1 small cauliflower, cut into florets
100 g (4 oz) fresh peas
A few leaves of fresh spinach, shredded
1 tablespoon plain flour
600 ml (1 pint) milk
1 tablespoon fresh parsley and dill, chopped

CHESTNUT BROTH WITH SOFT SPICES

SERVES

—— 4 ——

1 carrot, peeled and
  chopped
1 leek, chopped
2 sticks celery, chopped
A little vegetable oil for
  frying
½ teaspoon grated nutmeg
½ teaspoon ground
  cinnamon
½ teaspoon ground
  coriander
½ teaspoon mace
900 ml (1½ pints) water
1 ripe tomato, chopped, or
  1 tablespoon tomato
  passata (see page 16)
225 g (8 oz) peeled
  chestnuts, roughly
  chopped
300 ml (10 fl oz) milk
A few drops of lemon juice
Salt and pepper

Chestnuts have a bland, sweet taste which I don't always find appealing, however, the few drops of lemon juice and spicing in this soup balance the flavour nicely.

You can buy chestnuts ready peeled in vacuum packs which saves the tiresome business of roasting and peeling them. Should you find only tinned chestnuts, make sure that they are unsweetened.

Fry the carrot, leek and celery in the vegetable oil until they start to colour then stir in all the spices. Let the spices cook for a few seconds then add the water, and tomato or tomato passata. Stir well.

Add the chestnuts and boil until soft, around 20 minutes.

Add the milk, lemon juice and season to taste with salt and pepper.

Purée in batches in a liquidiser or food processor.

Return the soup to the pan to heat through before serving.

PEA AND MINT SOUP

S E R V E S

—— 4 ——

Frozen peas are an acceptable substitute for fresh peas. The flavour is delicate so don't use stock.

Melt the butter and cook the leek, without colouring, until slightly softened but not browned.

Add the lettuce leaves and stir until they become soft.

Add the water and bring to the boil. Simmer for 10 minutes, stirring occasionally.

Stir in the peas and bring back to the boil.

Add the mint and purée the soup in batches in a liquidiser. Check the seasoning and add salt and pepper to taste. If the soup is too thick or has over-reduced, add some warm milk.

INGREDIENTS

50 g (2 oz) unsalted butter
1 medium leek, sliced
1 small lettuce
600 ml (1 pint) water
450 g (1 lb) shelled or
 frozen peas
1 tablespoon chopped fresh
 mint
Salt and pepper

PASTA

Now that you can buy fresh pasta as readily as dried it is possible to compare the two products rationally and decide which is more appropriate to a dish.

Fresh pasta is soft and perishable. Whilst it may come in a rainbow of colours it is unlikely to be made into as many shapes as dried. It cooks quickly and has been a very welcome addition to our range of possibilities.

I have not worked out why it should cost so much more. Perhaps the packaging and shelf-life problems make it more expensive to handle. On the other hand maybe we are being overcharged because this is still a novelty product.

Dried pasta is the Cinderella of Italian food here. It is versatile, keeps practically indefinitely and can be cooked *al dente*, just cooked but still firm. While I know that the recipe for all shapes of pasta is virtually identical, I also know that farfalle (bow ties) and fusilli (corkscrews) taste very different from spaghettini or tagliatelle.

Use whichever suits your purse or fancy. Should anyone turn up their nose at your spaghetti tell them you prefer the traditional methods of manufacture and preserving. Alternatively tell them something ruder.

CONTENTS

TAGLIATELLE
WITH RED PEPPERS
AND CHEDDAR SAUCE

S E R V E S
— 4 —

The array of names for pasta is quite baffling. To make things worse tagliatelle is also sold as fettucine or even just as ribbon noodles. I'm sure it is not vital to the dish if you choose a slightly wider or thinner variety.

Red peppers go well with cheese. Cheddar may seem a bit incongruous in a pasta dish but in fact suits it fine. It is not our fault if Italians weren't lucky enough to have access to the splendour of mature Cheddar long enough ago for it to become traditional in Italian cooking.

Boil the pasta in salted water until just cooked then drain and keep warm.

Cut the peppers into 1 cm (½ inch) squares.

Fry the shallot, peppers and garlic in olive oil until they start to colour. Add the water and bring to the boil. Simmer for 5 minutes.

Use a slotted spoon to pick out just under half the pepper squares and keep on one side.

Liquidise the remainder with half the cheese. Add a few drops of lemon juice and several drops of chilli sauce. Return the sauce to the pan.

Add the spring onions to the pasta and toss with the remaining cheese and the reserved pieces of red pepper.

Check the seasoning in the sauce and add salt and pepper to taste. Pour the sauce over the pasta and serve.

INGREDIENTS

350 g (12 oz) tagliatelle (ribbon pasta)
2 red peppers, halved and de-seeded
1 shallot, peeled
1 clove garlic, peeled
1 tablespoon olive oil
150 ml (5 fl oz) water
100 g (4 oz) mature Cheddar cheese, grated
Lemon juice
Chilli sauce
4 spring onions, chopped
Salt and pepper

*F*USILLI WITH COURGETTES AND SUMMER HERBS

S E R V E S
—— 4 ——

350 g (12 oz) dried fusilli
(corkscrew-shaped pasta)
2 medium courgettes, sliced
into thin rounds
4 tablespoons good olive oil
2 large cloves of garlic,
crushed
2 ripe tomatoes
100 g (4 oz) Mozzarella
cheese
1 tablespoon chopped basil
1 tablespoon chopped
parsley
Juice of ½ lemon
Salt and pepper

Courgettes are available year round but are not equally good year round. Summer is the time when they are best.

This combination of courgette, summer herbs and thick, corkscrew pasta is filling without being heavy or cloying. In late spring or early summer you could substitute asparagus for the courgettes. As far as herbs are concerned, parsley should be plentiful that early but basil will be rather expensive.

Boil the fusilli in plenty of salted water until *al dente*.

Fry the courgettes in half the olive oil for about 3 or 4 minutes, until almost cooked. Add the garlic.

Cut the tomatoes and Mozzarella cheese into cubes. Mix these with the courgettes, chopped herbs, lemon juice and remaining olive oil. Season with a little salt and pepper.

Drain the fusilli and dress with the herbs and courgette mixture.

PASTA WITH BROCCOLI AND GORGONZOLA CHEESE SAUCE

S E R V E S

—— 4 ——

Blue cheese sauce is wonderful with pasta. Gorgonzola is best but the Irish Cashel Blue also works well. If neither is available use Dolcelatte. If you have no broccoli, use cauliflower. Don't waste the stalks, treated properly (see page 112, Broccoli Stalks Stir-fry) they are the best part.

Should you want to make your own pasta this is not difficult, 225 g (8 oz) plain flour and 2 eggs worked together then rested and thinly rolled will do the trick. Decent fresh pasta is available almost everywhere if you prefer to concentrate your efforts on the blue cheese sauce or if you can't wait for the 2 hours it takes for the pasta dough to be sufficiently worked and rested for cooking.

———

Cut the broccoli into florets. Trim the stalks and cut into 5 mm (¼ inch) pieces. Boil until tender in salted water then lift out with a slotted spoon.

Boil the pasta until cooked. You can use the broccoli water if there is enough. In any case you don't need to dirty another pot.

Bring the wine to a boil in a saucepan and boil steadily for a few minutes until it has reduced by half. Remove the pan from direct heat and stir in the cheese so that it melts and heats through but doesn't cook.

Drain the fresh pasta and add to the wine and cheese sauce. Mill plenty of black pepper and add the chopped walnuts and broccoli. Stir until the pasta is well coated and everything is heated through and then serve. Some chopped parsley will make it look attractive.

INGREDIENTS

275 g (10 oz) broccoli
225 g (8 oz) fresh pasta,
  preferably tagliatelle
120 ml (4 fl oz) dry white
  wine
100 g (4 oz) blue cheese,
  cubed
Black pepper
25 g (1 oz) walnuts,
  chopped
Fresh parsley, to garnish

BOW-TIE PASTA WITH PEAS AND SAFFRON

SERVES

— 4 —

INGREDIENTS

225 g (8 oz) bow-tie pasta
(farfalle)
25 g (1 oz) butter
¼ teaspoon saffron
150 ml (5 fl oz) double
cream
225 g (8 oz) shelled or
frozen peas
Salt and pepper
75 g (3 oz) Parmesan or
Pecorino cheese, grated

S affron is not only expensive, it is a powerful flavouring which needs using with care. More does not necessarily mean better and it can be a bullying ingredient, swamping all other tastes, if sprinkled on too generously.

Should you particularly like the yellow colour it gives, add a pinch of turmeric or an edible colouring. That way the balance of flavouring and the delicacy of the peas won't be lost.

Bring a large, covered saucepan of salted water to the boil and add the pasta. Stir and reboil.

As the bow-ties cook, melt the butter with the saffron in a separate saucepan. Let this cook for a few seconds then pour on the cream and stir. After a minute or two the sauce will turn pale yellow. Do not allow the sauce to boil but heat it through gently.

When the pasta is at the *al dente* stage add the peas to the pasta pot and cook for 2 minutes.

Drain the pasta and peas and season with salt and pepper. Toss them in the saffron sauce and serve topped with the cheese.

Main Courses

Vegetable main courses can fail to satisfy. Portions need to be generous or there will be a sense that something is missing from the meal.

The most important reason for serving vegetables should be because they taste good and you enjoy them not purely because you want to impose an environmental or nutritional standpoint on your friends and family.

Anyone with palate enough to tell the difference will enjoy well-prepared vegetable dishes and appreciate seeing them centre-stage. Most people are eating less meat in their routine diet anyway and no one should want to eat meat or farmed fish unless they are sure the animals have been properly reared, decently fed and humanely killed. If we need to eat less animal protein in order to see the end of battery farming and hormone implants, so much the better. The range of vegetables gets wider all the time.

Sadly, vegetables do not yet get a completely clean bill of health on the ecological front either. Chemical residues from pesticide sprays mean you must wash any vegetable that you intend using as a crudité or in salads. Also some countries permit the irradiation of soft fruit as a method of preservation. Luckily, these out of season raspberries and strawberries don't taste good anyway so you may solve this problem by avoiding them.

CONTENTS

WONTONS

S E R V E S

—— 20 ——

Wontons are often used as soup garnish. Fried, they are much more exciting and can be served as a snack or starter. As a main course I would serve them in a mixed salad with a dressing of light sesame oil and rice vinegar.

———————

Heat the groundnut oil in a frying-pan or wok then fry the ginger and garlic until they colour.

Add all the other filling ingredients and cook for 1 minute then empty into a bowl to cool for a few seconds.

Fill the Wontons. Place a wrapper in front of you in a diamond position. Drop a good teaspoonful of filling in the centre then moisten all four edges. Pull the top corner down to the bottom corner, folding the wrapper over into a triangle. Press the edges together. If the filling looks in danger of escaping, draw the corners of the triangle up above the filling. Moisten and press together. All should now be secure. Dust with a little cornflour and move on to the next wrapper.

Heat oil to a depth of 2.5 cm (1 inch) in a wok or deep frying-pan and deep fry the wontons in batches.

Drain briefly on kitchen paper before serving.

INGREDIENTS

20 Wonton wrappers
A little cornflour
Saucer of water

FOR THE FILLING
2 tablespoons groundnut oil
1 tablespoon fresh ginger, grated
1 clove garlic, crushed
6 spring onions, chopped
1 tablespoon dark sesame oil
1 tablespoon soy sauce
1 red pepper, very finely chopped
4 asparagus spears, very finely chopped
Oil for frying

COURGETTE RISOTTO WITH PARMESAN CHEESE SAUCE

SERVES

— 4 —

INGREDIENTS

FOR THE RISOTTO
50 g (2 oz) butter
1 medium onion, peeled
   and chopped
225 g (8 oz) Arborio rice
Salt and pepper
150 ml (5 fl oz) white
   wine
900 ml (1½ pints)
   vegetable stock (see page
   41)
A pinch of saffron

450 g (1 lb) courgettes
Fresh chives, to garnish
   (optional)

FOR THE SAUCE
150 ml (5 fl oz) vegetable
   stock (page 30)
1 clove of garlic, chopped
25 g (1 oz) fresh Parmesan
   cheese, grated
50 ml (2 fl oz) olive oil
Squeeze of lemon
Pepper

Risotto is best made with the Arborio variety of rice. Any packet headed 'Italian Risotto Rice' will almost certainly be Arborio and do the job well. There is more to risotto than choosing the rice variety though: the cooking procedure is different from pilaff or boiled rice.

This recipe calls for wine, saffron and vegetable stock. The wine and saffron are optional but if you substitute water for stock the results will be rather dull. Take care if you use bouillon cube to make the stock as the amount of boiling involved could build up a nasty concentration of salts, especially when cheese is to be added.

At the end of cooking, the rice should be slightly firm and there should be plenty of cheese and buttery liquid. Courgettes suit risotto particularly well, as would asparagus, artichokes or mushrooms.

Melt 25 g (1 oz) butter and cook the onion for 3 minutes without colouring. The onion should no longer smell raw but should not be browned. Add the rice and continue cooking for another 3 minutes.

Season with salt and pepper then add the wine. Let the wine reduce right away, stirring occasionally to prevent the rice sticking. This will take only 3 or 4 minutes.

Add 300 ml (10 fl oz) stock and reboil. If you are not intending to eat straightaway you may turn off the heat and leave the rice to absorb the stock. It will then be three-quarters cooked and may be completed 10 minutes before you wish to eat. Once the risotto is completely cooked it needs to be eaten straightaway otherwise residual heat will overcook the grains and leave you with something resembling rice pudding.

When the rice has absorbed the stock add another 300 ml (10 fl oz) and reboil. When this has been absorbed add the final 300 ml (10 fl oz) and reboil.

When this has been almost completely absorbed remove the pan from the heat and stir in 25 g (1 oz) butter and a pinch of saffron.

Meanwhile, cook the courgettes and make the sauce. Top and tail the courgettes. Peel off alternate strips of skin, then slice into rounds. Boil these for 3 to 4 minutes in salted water and then drain. They should be firm but cooked. Season them with salt and pepper.

Make the sauce by heating the stock with the garlic, cheese and olive oil. Liquidise and then finish the sauce with a squeeze of lemon. Check the seasoning, you may want some pepper but shouldn't need salt.

Spoon the risotto into soup bowls. Pour on the sauce then scatter the courgettes on top. You may garnish with more Parmesan cheese or chopped chives if you fancy.

GRATIN OF JERUSALEM ARTICHOKES

S E R V E S

— 4 —

INGREDIENTS

1 kg (2 lb) Jerusalem
 artichokes
Salt
50 g (2 oz) butter
25 g (1 oz) plain flour
450 ml (15 fl oz) milk
3 egg yolks
175 g (6 oz) Parmesan
 cheese, grated
Ground black pepper

These knobbly tubers are neither artichokes nor in anyway connected with Jerusalem. The name comes from a corruption of girasole, the Italian for sunflower to which they are related and from the flavour which is similar to artichoke.

Smooth, firm specimens are best and can be roasted, fried or puréed like potato. They have an unfortunate reputation for causing wind – if you know what I mean.

Preheat the oven to Gas Mark 8, 230°C (450°F).

Wash the artichokes then cook for 15 minutes in boiling, salted water by which time they should be tender. Drain and as soon as the vegetables are cool enough peel them.

Meanwhile melt the butter and stir in the flour. Let this cook for a few seconds then add the milk gradually, stirring all the time. Bring to the boil.

Remove from the heat and stir in the egg yolks and two-thirds of the Parmesan cheese. Season to taste.

Slice the Jerusalem artichokes and place in an oven-proof dish. Spoon the sauce over the top. Sprinkle on the remaining Parmesan cheese.

Bake in the oven for 15 minutes.

LEEK AND POTATO HASH WITH POACHED EGG

SERVES
— 4 —

This is an easy dish. Its swiftness, however, depends on your refrigerator containing some ready-baked potatoes. If unaccountably it does not, you will have to cook some in advance. Perhaps this is the moment to use a microwave, should you own one.

───────

When the potatoes are cold, peel and shred them, discarding the skins.

Melt the butter in a saucepan and fry the onion and leeks until they are soft. This should take only 5 minutes and it doesn't matter if they colour a little. Mix the onion and leeks with the potatoes. Season well.

Heat a frying-pan and add some vegetable oil. When this is hot add the hash mixture so that it is around 1 cm (½ inch) deep and covers most of the pan. Leave a 2.5 cm (1 inch) space all round between the hash and the frying-pan's rim. Cook in batches if your pan isn't large enough. Turn the hash over half-way through cooking.

When the hash is brown and crunchy, after about 10 minutes, lift it out on to a dish or tray. This is best achieved by loosening the hash with a spatula or egg slice, placing the dish over the pan then inverting it. If your pan is small you will need to keep the first batch of hash warm in the oven while you repeat the process.

While the hash cooks, poach the eggs. Bring a saucepan of salted water to the boil. Crack each egg in turn into a saucer and then gently slide it into the water. Just 2 minutes later the poached eggs should be perfect and can be lifted out with a slotted spoon, dried on a piece of kitchen paper and placed on a portion of hash to serve.

It isn't necessary to add vinegar to the poaching water unless you particularly like its flavour. There is an old wives' tale about the vinegar helping the egg white to coagulate. In fact all it does is spoil the flavour of the egg and drip over the hash.

INGREDIENTS

*4 large potatoes, baked in
   their jackets and cooled
25 g (1 oz) butter
1 medium onion, peeled
   and sliced
4 medium leeks, cut into
   2.5 cm (1 inch) pieces
   (see page 83)
Salt and black pepper
Vegetable oil for frying
4 eggs*

FILO PASTRY PIE WITH SPINACH AND FRESH GOAT'S CHEESE

SERVES
— 4 —

8 sheets filo pastry (about a quarter of a standard packet)
A little olive oil
450 g (1 lb) fresh spinach
Nutmeg, salt, pepper
1 × 175 g (6 oz) fresh goat's cheese, e.g. Perroche, Cabri, Chevrefeuille

One of the West Country's finest pubs, the Double Locks in Alphington, serves a creditable version of this dish using feta cheese (Greek sheep's-milk cheese).

Filo pastry seemed to arrive on the scene in the 1980s. It's certainly not new though. Pastry cooks in Greece have been making similar confections since Old Testament times and the Roman writer Pliny gave a detailed recipe in the first century A.D.

It dries very quickly if exposed to air so always keep it wrapped either in its original plastic or else between damp cloths.

Preheat the oven to Gas Mark 7, 220°C (425°F).

Brush each sheet of pastry on both sides with olive oil.

Lay the sheets so that they overlap, four deep in a 25 cm (10 in) tart case. The pastry should spread well beyond the rim of the tart case for you are going to fold it back across the top of the filling to form the pie's top crust.

Boil the spinach briefly and press out as much moisture as possible. Season with a small amount of salt and plenty of nutmeg and pepper. Remember the cheese will be salty.

Put half the spinach into the pie and spread it over the base.

Next arrange a layer of goat cheese slices on top.

Spread the remaining spinach on top then tuck in the pastry across the top of the pie. Cut off any excess.

Bake in the oven for 20 minutes or until golden brown and flaky.

PARSLEY AND SPRING ONION TART IN WALNUT PASTRY

SERVES

—— 4 ——

If you intend to make the pastry in advance, which is the ideal for any dish that involves lining a tart case, you will find the walnut pastry much easier to handle. I haven't come across walnut pastry for sale so I can't offer the alternative of buying it instead, I'm afraid. Most shop pastry is basically OK but manufacturers tend for commercial reasons to skimp on expensive or short shelf-life ingredients. It's worth studying the ingredients list on the packet and sticking to a reliable brand if you find one.

Make the pastry. The butter should be at room temperature rather than straight from the refrigerator. Mix the butter and egg together with a pinch of salt. It will look awful but don't despair.

Stir in the flour and ground walnuts. Knead once or twice to make sure all the ingredients are mixed then refrigerate for about 30 minutes.

Preheat the oven to Gas Mark 6, 200°C (400°F).

Make the filling by whisking all the ingredients together.

Roll out the pastry and line a 25 cm (10 inch) greased flan tin. Bake blind in the oven for 15 minutes.

Pour in the filling and bake for a further 30 minutes or until the top is golden brown and the filling is set but not solid. Serve warm.

INGREDIENTS

FOR THE PASTRY
175 g (6 oz) unsalted butter
1 small egg
Salt
150 g (5 oz) plain flour
100 g (4 oz) ground walnuts

FOR THE FILLING
3 eggs and 1 yolk
175 ml (6 fl oz) milk
175 ml (6 fl oz) double cream
1 heaped tablespoon chopped parsley
6 spring onions, chopped
Nutmeg, pepper, salt

SCRAMBLED EGGS WITH RUNNER BEANS, PARSLEY AND GARLIC

SERVES

—— 4 ——

INGREDIENTS

225 g (8 oz) runner beans
1 clove garlic, crushed
1 tablespoon olive oil
Salt and pepper
8 eggs
100 g (4 oz) cream cheese,
* cut into small cubes*
1 tablespoon chopped
* parsley*
French bread, to serve.

Ever since the hysteria a few years ago over salmonella in low-quality battery eggs, many people have been overcooking dishes such as fried or scrambled eggs. If salmonella is a worry to you, my advice is to purchase free-range eggs from a trustworthy supermarket or supplier. If you are using them as the centre of a meal rather than, say, an ingredient in a cake they still represent good value.

The guidelines on timing for cooking items such as summer beans are no more than that – guidelines. Early-season specimens that are thin and tender will cook in 3 minutes. Large, coarse ones may take twice that time. Your best bet, if unsure, is to lift one out with a fork when you think it may be done, cut off a small piece, and eat it.

───────

String the beans and boil in salted water until tender, about 3–5 minutes.

Drain and cut into 5 mm (¼ inch) pieces.

Heat the garlic in the olive oil for a few seconds then add the beans and season with salt and pepper.

When the beans are coated with the garlic and olive oil add all the remaining ingredients.

Cook over a moderate heat, drawing a wooden spoon continuously across the bottom of the saucepan to produce large, soft curds of scrambled egg and cheese. Serve on the creamy side, with some toasted slices of French bread.

Opposite: CARROT TIMBALE (*page 38*)
Overleaf: COUSCOUS WITH HOT SPICED RAGOÛT (*page 72*)

POACHED NEW SEASON LEEKS AND POTATOES IN WELSH RAREBIT SAUCE

S E R V E S

— 4 —

The taste and texture of Welsh Rarebit is handy for more than spreading on toast. The bite added by mustard and Worcestershire sauce goes nicely with the solid, earthy flavours of potato and leek.

———

Boil the potatoes for 12–15 minutes until done. Drain and cut into 5 mm (¼ inch) slices.

Wash the leeks carefully (see page 83) and cut into 5 cm (2 inch) lengths. Boil for 3 to 4 minutes until tender. Drain well.

Arrange the leeks and potatoes in a shallow ovenproof dish. Season with a little salt and pepper.

Preheat the grill.

Melt the butter in a saucepan then stir in the flour. Cook for a few seconds over a low heat.

Add the milk and stir until completely blended.

Add the mustard and Worcestershire sauce. Bring to the boil.

Remove the pan from the heat and stir in the cheese and then the egg yolks.

Spoon this mixture over the leeks and potato then place under the grill until the top is golden brown and the sauce is bubbling.

INGREDIENTS

450 g (1 lb) new potatoes, scrubbed
450 g (1 lb) small new season leeks
Salt and pepper
25 g (1 oz) butter
15 g (½ oz) plain flour
50 ml (2 fl oz) milk
1 tablespoon mustard
3 dashes Worcestershire sauce
225 g (8 oz) Cheddar cheese, grated
2 egg yolks, beaten

Opposite: BITTER SALADS WITH WARM ASPARAGUS AND SESAME DRESSING (*page 94*)

Preceding page: FUSILLI WITH COURGETTES AND SUMMER HERBS (*page 54*)

COUSCOUS WITH HOT SPICED VEGETABLE RAGOÛT

SERVES

— 4 —

FOR THE COUSCOUS
225 g (8 oz) couscous
250 ml (8 fl oz) water
15 g (½ oz) butter
Salt, ground cinnamon

FOR THE RAGOÛT
4 carrots, peeled and sliced
100 g (4 oz) chick peas,
*   tinned or soaked in water*
*   overnight*
8 small onions, peeled
450 g (1 lb) runner beans,
*   stringed and cut into*
*   1 cm (½ inch) pieces*
1 green or red pepper,
*   de-seeded and cut into*
*   1 cm (½ inch) pieces*
4 courgettes, cut into 1 cm
*   (½ inch) slices*
Salt
A few fresh coriander
*   leaves*
1 tablespoon tomato passata
1 teaspoon paprika
1 teaspoon chilli sauce or ½
*   teaspoon cayenne pepper*

Couscous is a Berber dish from the Maghreb countries of North Africa. The grains are milled from wheat like semolina and it is traditionally steamed in the top half of a device called a couscoussier. I have never seen anything other than precooked couscous on sale, which makes it a simple and tasty alternative to rice or pasta.

The ingredients for the ragoût are a guideline. Use what is best, and to hand. Broad beans and peas are especially good if you have time to shell them, or a child who can be bribed to do the job.

If your delicatessen or supermarket sells harissa, a fiery red pepper paste from North Africa, buy it to use instead of chilli in this dish.

Make the couscous. Put the couscous into a largish bowl, pour on the cold water and mix in thoroughly.

Leave for 15 minutes. The couscous will absorb the water and swell up. Stir occasionally.

Heat the butter in a frying-pan and add the couscous. Initially it may stick a little. Keep stirring until it is hot, the grains dry and separate.

Season with salt and a pinch of cinnamon.

This method will work well but if you have a steamer or double saucepan that can serve as one you can preheat the couscous before adding the water. Place it in a sieve or strainer and heat it through in steam before adding the cold water. Leave for 15 minutes to absorb the water, as before. Then you will need to return the couscous to the steamer to heat through, of course. Either method will produce good results.

To make the ragout, bring a pint of water to the boil then add the carrots, chick peas and onions. If the onions are large, halve them. If small, leave them whole. Pick-ling onions are ideal. Ten minutes later add the runner beans and pepper then finally the courgettes. Cover the saucepan with a lid and cook for 5 minutes. Add a good pinch of salt.

Add the coriander, tomato passata, paprika and chilli sauce and stir well. If you are nervous about how much chilli or cayenne pepper to add, lift out a small ladleful of cooking liquor and add it gradually to that, testing for hotness before returning it to the pan. Serve with the couscous.

ALSATIAN ONION TART

S E R V E S

—— 4 ——

INGREDIENTS

FOR THE PASTRY
100 g (4 oz) plain flour
50 g (2 oz) butter, softened
1 egg
Salt

FOR THE FILLING
750 g (1½ lb) onions,
  peeled and sliced
3 egg yolks
175 ml (6 fl oz) double
  cream
Nutmeg, salt and pepper
25 g (1 oz) butter
A little vegetable oil for
  frying

Make or buy the pastry. Quicker if you buy, better if you make.

Preheat the oven to Gas Mark 6, 200°C (400°F).

If you are making pastry do so by whisking the egg and butter together with a pinch of salt, stirring in the flour and then kneading the resulting dough four or five times until smooth.

Melt the butter and heat with the oil. Stew the onions in this until fully cooked, but not browned. A lid will speed the process along.

Mix the egg yolks, cream, salt, pepper and nutmeg together then combine with the cooked onion.

Roll out the pastry and line a 25 cm (10 inch) greased flan tin.

Pour in the onion mixture and bake in the oven for 30 minutes or until cooked and brown on top. The filling should be just set. Serve warm.

TIAN OF AUBERGINES

S E R V E S

—— 4 ——

Tian is part of that collection of words like timbale or casserole which define a dish by the pot in which it is cooked or served rather than some aspect of the flavouring or cooking process.

A tian is an earthenware dish from Provence with a wide rim tapering quickly to a narrow base, thus giving a good ratio of crisp gratinated topping to rather less filling. By association a tian is any vegetable dish cooked this way.

INGREDIENTS

1 kg (2 lb) aubergines
Salt
1 tablespoon lemon juice
450 g (1 lb) sun-dried
    tomatoes, chopped
1 bunch of fresh basil,
    chopped
225 g (8 oz) Gruyère
    cheese, grated

Preheat the oven to Gas Mark 4, 180°C (350°F).

Slice the aubergine into rounds and sprinkle with a good pinch of salt.

Bring a saucepan of water to the boil. Add the lemon juice and aubergine slices and boil for 1 minute. Drain well.

Layer the aubergine slices alternately with the tomatoes in a greased ovenproof dish. Use a tian-shaped dish if you have one but other shapes will also work.

Top with the basil and Gruyère cheese then bake in the oven for 40 minutes. Serve hot.

CAPONATA

(SICILIAN VEGETABLE STEW)

SERVES

—— 4 ——

INGREDIENTS

1 kg (2 lb) aubergines
Salt and pepper
1 head of celery
Vegetable oil for frying
1 tablespoon sugar
2 tablespoons wine vinegar
1 × 450 g (1 lb) jar of
  tomato passata or 1 ×
  400 g (14 oz) tin
  chopped plum tomatoes
50 g (2 oz) capers
100 g (4 oz) pitted green
  olives
1 tablespoon chopped fresh
  parsley

Sicily was the home of gastronomy in classical times and the Greek cities on the island produced the most sought-after chefs in the Mediterranean for many centuries. This may seem a rather grandiose fanfare for this celery and aubergine stew. It's good to remember sometimes, however, that superficially unlikely places can have immaculate culinary pedigrees. Al Capone was not Sicily's only export.

Cut the aubergine into large dice. Lightly dust with salt and leave them on kitchen paper. The salt will make them weep out a little liquid but reduces any bitterness in the vegetable.

Peel away the coarse outside stalks of the celery and then cut the rest into 1 cm (½ inch) slices. Boil these in salted water for 10 minutes. Drain well.

Deep-fry the aubergines. This will only take a few minutes.

Melt the sugar and vinegar together then bring them to the boil. Add the tomato passata or tomatoes – this is best done with the saucepan away from direct heat as it may spatter. Season with salt and pepper to taste.

Add the celery and aubergine. Cook gently for 30 minutes.

Stir in the capers, olives and parsley. Serve hot or cold.

LATE SUMMER VEGETABLE RAGOÛT

S E R V E S

— 4 —

You will need two pots for this. The vegetables are a guideline, you may use less, more or different ones as it suits you.

———

Bring a pot of salted water to the boil. Separately heat 300 ml (10 fl oz) of water and just a pinch of salt in a wide lidded saucepan or a deep frying-pan. Add the onions to this pan and simmer for 5 minutes.

Next boil the carrots in the first pot for 1 minute and transfer them with a slotted spoon to the pan with the onions.

Then boil the broccoli, courgettes and sweetcorn in the first pot for 2 minutes. Transfer these over to the second pot. You may need to also add a little more water.

Finally cook the beans in the first pot for 2 minutes and then transfer these to the second pot.

Cover the pan and boil for 5 minutes. Check that the water hasn't all evaporated and, if necessary, add a little: you should end up with around 200 ml (7 fl oz) of liquid. Uncover the pan and stir in the herbs, garlic and butter, tossing the vegetables in the liquid. Season with salt and pepper then serve.

INGREDIENTS

8 small pickling onions or shallots, peeled
12 baby carrots, peeled
1 head of broccoli, cut into florets
6 small courgettes, quartered
8 baby sweetcorns
12 green french beans, topped and tailed
1 tablespoon chopped mixed herbs
1 clove garlic, chopped
50 g (2 oz) butter
Salt and pepper

SALADS

Lettuces and chicories can provide a bowlful of colours ranging from dark-green corn salad through oakleaf lettuce's browns and bronze to radicchio's bright purple. The flavours cover an equally wide spectrum so take care to choose a combination which will balance.

The most bitter come from the chicory family. In moderation they will provide a marvellous astringency to your salad, too much can be like grazing a hedgerow. Most varieties have come to us from northern Italy and are naturally winter salads. All now appear to have become available year round though. Mostly this is good news, increasing the choice for us shoppers. I hope the apparent edging out of superb lettuces like Cos or Webb's Wonder is only temporary until the novelty of multi-coloured leaves wears off.

One or two other leaves have also become more accessible. Rocket, which has a peppery, radish-like flavour, is enjoying a vogue because of its popularity in American–Italian salad dishes where it goes by the Italian name Arugula.

And dandelion leaves, usually a viciously bitter salad, are now occasionally on offer blanched, their flavour and texture transformed into an almost nutty crispness.

Some of the names for these lettuces have not quite settled. Frizzy (or frisée) endive is also called curly endive, and corn salad can be sold as lamb's lettuce or *salade de mâche*. Confused? Of course not. If you have any doubts buy a pack of mixed leaves and then try to remember which you prefer.

There are a few ground rules to successful salad making. Wash the lettuces in very cold water if you can for it helps them regain crispness. Don't leave them for long periods in water though.

Once washed, shake the leaves as dry as possible. Otherwise residual water will dilute the dressing. Finally toss the salad in dressing, including mayonnaise or salad cream if that's what you are using. Use a large bowl and turn the salad over 4 or 5 times so that the leaves are thinly and evenly covered.

CONTENTS

BASIC
SALAD DRESSINGS

Mayonnaise is easy to make. So is salad cream and both have the bonus of being vastly superior to any of the commercial preparations on offer. Dressings like mayonnaise which use raw egg yolk have a limited shelf-life, even in a refrigerator. They keep better than plain raw eggs only because the vinegar in the recipe changes the pH (acidity) level, thus retarding bacterial growth. Even so I wouldn't advise you to keep mayonnaise for more than a couple of days. Best to make the amount you are going to need and use the remainder in late-night snacks of salad sandwiches. Dutch people are alleged to eat mayonnaise with chips; you could find out whether this idea is better than it sounds.

──────

All ingredients should be at room temperature.

Put the egg yolks in a bowl with the mustard, vinegar and some salt and pepper. Stir well.

Whisk in the oil, at first in a small trickle then, as it thickens, a little faster. Test for seasoning. Add more salt, pepper or vinegar as needed.

If it curdles it will almost certainly be because it is too thick. Whisk in, or blend in, some lukewarm water. If all else fails begin with another yolk and beat in the curdled mixture.

INGREDIENTS

2 egg yolks, beaten
1 teaspoon Dijon mustard
1 tablespoon white wine
  vinegar
Salt and pepper
150 ml (5 fl oz) olive oil
150 ml (5 fl oz) groundnut
  oil

SALAD CREAM

INGREDIENTS

2 hard-boiled eggs
Salt and pepper
A pinch of cayenne pepper
  or dash of chilli sauce
1 teaspoon water
1 teaspoon mustard
1 teaspoon caster sugar
150 ml (5 fl oz) double
  cream
Juice of 1 lemon

Separate the hard-boiled eggs into yolks and white. Chop the white and keep it to one side to mix into the sauce at the end.

Make a paste of the yolks and seasonings, sugar and water.

Incorporate the cream by trickling it on to the paste, stirring or whisking constantly.

Add lemon juice and decorate with the chopped egg whites.

OLIVE OIL DRESSING

INGREDIENTS

2 parts olive oil
1 part groundnut oil
1 part wine vinegar
Salt and pepper

Either whisk together or liquidise in a blender just before serving.

Use the best olive oil you can afford (see pages 15–16), and one which will suit the salad you are preparing.

LEEKS IN VINAIGRETTE

SERVES

—— 4 ——

Cleaning leeks properly demands as much attention as the rest of the recipe which is straightforward. Unfortunately leeks are prone to catching large amounts of grit and soil between their layers. This needs removing completely if your dish is to be a pleasure rather than an experience.

Trim the green portion of the leaves so that any tough parts are removed. Then trim the root, cutting away any bristles or fibres attached to its top but leaving enough to hold the leek layers intact. Insert a sharp knife, with blade pointing downwards, just below the tip of the root and slice down through the vegetable. It should be cut almost in half but still held together by the top of the white root. Wash the leek under running water. You should be able to peel back the layers and clean it thoroughly without any difficulty.

Prepare and wash the leeks. Drop them in boiling, salted water and cook until tender. This should take around 10 minutes, though obviously the timing will vary with the size of vegetables and volume of the saucepan.

When they are done, lift out the leeks and run cold water over them. This stops the cooking process and also preserves any bright green colour on the leaves.

Make a vinaigrette dressing by mixing the Dijon mustard and vinegar, seasoning with salt and pepper and whisking in the oil, a trickle at a time. The vinaigrette will emulsify and thicken as you add the oil. You will find that adding a tablespoon of the cooking water from the leeks will make the dressing more stable. Should the vinaigrette separate, just whisk it back together before serving. The reason for emulsifying the dressing is to make sure the ratio of oil to vinegar and seasoning is evenly distributed.

Turn the leeks in the vinaigrette and serve barely warm.

INGREDIENTS

8 small or medium-sized
  leeks
1 tablespoon Dijon mustard
1 tablespoon wine vinegar
Salt and pepper
300 ml (10 fl oz)
  groundnut oil

83

SPINACH AND AVOCADO SALAD

SERVES

—— 4 ——

350 g (12 oz) raw spinach
1 ripe avocado, peeled and
  sliced
2 hard-boiled eggs,
  quartered
3 slices of white bread,
  5 mm (¼ inch) thick
4 tablespoons olive oil
1 teaspoon white wine
  vinegar
1 tablespoon Dijon
  Mustard
Salt and black pepper

Young, tender spinach leaves are essential to this salad. If there are none available, make something else. Old, discoloured leaves will be too coarse to eat raw and of course it would be entirely inappropriate to use frozen spinach.

Wash and sort through the spinach. Discard any stalks or leaves which aren't tender. Pat dry and put into a salad bowl with the avocado and eggs.

Cut the bread into cubes and fry in half the olive oil. Add to the salad.

Mix the vinegar and mustard together. Season with salt and black pepper then trickle in the remaining olive oil as you stir or whisk the dressing.

Toss the salad in the dressing and serve.

SAUERKRAUT AND BEETROOT SALAD WITH OLIVE OIL AND GARLIC

S E R V E S
—— 4 ——

Sauerkraut should not be unduly sour or salty; eating it after all is meant to be a pleasure. Brands vary, so after you have lifted the amount you want from the jar or tin, do taste it. Rinse off any excess brine and if it doesn't taste delicious rinse a second time in tepid water then press dry.

Cut the beetroot into cubes and mix with the sauerkraut.

Whisk the garlic and olive oil together and grind plenty of black pepper into it.

Toss the sauerkraut and beetroot in the dressing.

INGREDIENTS

225 g (8 oz) cooked beetroot
225 g (8 oz) sauerkraut
2 cloves garlic, crushed
4 tablespoons olive oil
Black pepper

HUNGARIAN CUCUMBER SALAD

SERVES

—— 4 ——

2 large cucumbers, peeled
and thinly sliced
Salt
1 tablespoon white wine
vinegar
1 tablespoon granulated
sugar
Black pepper
1 tablespoon soured cream
A sprig of fresh dill

You need a surprisingly large amount of cucumber per person for it loses volume after being salted. The peel doesn't suit this treatment so you will need to remove and discard it.

The only use for cucumber peel that I know of is as a garnish for Pimm's cocktail, an over-rated gin-based concoction which can be drunk on summer afternoons. I'm sure you don't need such a flimsy excuse for an afternoon's boozing but if you do this is your chance.

———

Toss the cucumber in a shallow bowl with 2 teaspoons of salt and place a weighted plate on top to draw out the juices. This should take only 30 minutes.

Meanwhile whisk together the vinegar, sugar and a little black pepper.

Wash and drain the cucumber slices, pressing them lightly to extract as much moisture as possible.

Toss the cucumber in the vinegar and sugar dressing then serve in a mound, with a tablespoon of soured cream and a sprig of dill for garnish.

CELERIAC SALAD WITH MUSTARD DRESSING

SERVES

— 4 —

Celeriac can be used cooked or raw in salads. Raw, it needs thinly shredding like carrot and is predominantly a celery-flavoured crunch. My preference is for cooked celeriac, the flavour comes through so much better.

Boil the celeriac in salted water with a few drops of lemon juice until tender. How long this takes will depend on the size of your celeriac cubes (1 cm or ½ in dice will take about 15 minutes). You can boil the celeriac whole and then peel and cube it if you prefer. This involves an hour's cooking however.

Make the dressing by whisking together the onion, mustard, cream and olive oil. Season with salt and pepper and sharpen with a little lemon juice.

Drain the celeriac and toss it in the dressing. Keep in the fridge. If left overnight the flavour develops even more.

INGREDIENTS

FOR THE SALAD
1 medium celeriac, peeled
and cubed
Salt
A little lemon juice

FOR THE DRESSING
1 small onion, peeled and
chopped
1 tablespoon English
mustard powder
90–120 ml (3–4 fl oz)
double cream
2 tablespoons olive oil
Salt and pepper

CRUDITÉS AND DIPS

**ALLOW 225 G
(8 OZ) PER PERSON**

*A selection from
Mange-touts, topped and
    tailed
Carrots, peeled and cut into
    sticks
Red, green or yellow
    peppers, in strips
Belgian endive, in leaves
Celery, peeled and cut into
    sticks
Cucumber, unpeeled and
    cut into sticks
Spring onions, trimmed
Radishes, trimmed
Button mushrooms, washed
    and quartered*

Not all vegetables make good crudités. Surprisingly, vegetables have a more muted taste when raw and need cooking in order to bring out their individual flavours. What is needed from a crudité ingredient is texture – preferably crispness or crunch. Carrots and celery are obvious candidates, sprouts and broccoli less so. Most root vegetables, celeriac is the exception, aren't particularly digestible raw, so no parsnips or swede. Too much raw veg will in any case be boring so if you plan to eat crudités and not much else it is an idea to include breadsticks or strips of dry toast amongst the vegetables.

How these are served is a matter of your personal aesthetics, small bundles of each ingredient in bowls or in jugs of iced water is fine.

Good dips are essential to the dish. A selection of two or three makes it more interesting. If you can buy good hummus, or cream cheese and herbs so much the better.

AVOCADO AND CHILLI DIP

*1 ripe avocado
1 tablespoon chopped coriander leaves
1 chilli, de-seeded and chopped (or use chilli sauce)
1 tablespoon lemon juice
2 tablespoons olive oil
Salt and pepper*

Chop, mash or purée together in a liquidiser. Serve as soon as possible to avoid the dip discolouring.

GARLIC MAYONNAISE

*4 cloves of garlic, crushed
300 ml (10 fl oz) mayonnaise (see page 81)*

Blend the garlic with the mayonnaise. This will keep for a couple of days in the refrigerator.

CAESAR SALAD

SERVES

— 4 —

With the rainbow of lettuces available, red, brown, curly and frizzy, it is easy to forget just how good Cos lettuce tastes. In this famous American salad it has the starring rôle. There are countless variations using different cheeses or chopped anchovy fillets.

Wash and drain the lettuce. Shake off any excess water or pat the leaves dry with a clean cloth. Residual water will dilute the dressing. Break the leaves into fairly large pieces in a bowl.

Crush the garlic with the salt then add the pepper, mustard and lemon juice. Beat in two-thirds of the olive oil (the rest will be used to fry the croutons).

Drop the eggs into boiling water for 1 minute.

Cut the bread into cubes and fry until crisp and golden brown. If your pan is large and the oil seems insufficient top up with vegetable or groundnut oil. If you prefer you can bake the bread cubes in the oil in a moderately hot oven (Gas Mark 5, 190°C, 375°F) until golden brown. Shake them regularly while baking.

Assemble the salad by tossing the leaves in the dressing. Crack the eggs into the salad and toss it again. Finally add the croutons, Parmesan cheese, and a dash of Worcestershire sauce, once more tossing the salad until all the dressing is coating the leaves.

INGREDIENTS

1 Cos lettuce
1 clove garlic
$\frac{1}{2}$ teaspoon salt
Black pepper
1 teaspoon Dijon mustard
Juice of 1 lemon
150 ml (5 fl oz) olive oil
2 eggs
3 slices of white bread, 5 mm ($\frac{1}{4}$ inch) thick
4 tablespoons Parmesan cheese, grated
Dash of Worcestershire sauce

COLD ROAST AUBERGINE SALAD WITH LEMON PEEL AND YOGHURT

SERVES
—— 4 ——

INGREDIENTS

1 kg (2 lb) aubergines
2 large cloves garlic, peeled
   and sliced
1 lemon
1 tablespoon olive oil
1 teaspoon chopped fresh
   mint
2 tablespoons natural
   yoghurt
Salt and pepper

You may need to approach this recipe with some flexibility. Aubergines are fairly large vegetables as a rule and it's best to use one large or two medium and adjust the remaining ingredients accordingly if the weight isn't spot on 1 kg (2 lb). Baking aubergines takes about an hour so do this in advance.

Preheat the oven to Gas Mark 6, 200°C (400°F). Make small cuts into the aubergine skin and insert a sliver of garlic into each cut.

Roast the aubergines in the oven for an hour until they are quite soft. Leave them on kitchen paper to cool completely.

Halve the aubergines and scoop out the flesh and garlic into a bowl. You don't need the skins.

Chop or mash this fairly finely. You can use a food processor if you wish although the amount of washing up created may not justify the chopping time saved.

Grate the lemon peel on to the chopped aubergine then stir in the olive oil, mint and yoghurt. Season with salt, pepper and a few drops of lemon juice.

Form into dumpling shapes (compress into quenelles between two dessertspoons) to serve. This is good accompanied by other salads and hot bread or toast.

COLD POACHED ASPARAGUS WITH PARSLEY PESTO

PER
PERSON

Young asparagus is unlikely to need peeling. Do cut off the bases of the stems though. As well as being woody they are likely to have fungus spores which will taint your meal. Boil the asparagus until tender, about 20–30 minutes. Lift out the asparagus and dunk it in cold water. This will stop the cooking process and preserve the natural colours of the asparagus. Save 120 ml (4 fl oz) of the cooking liquor and allow it to cool.

In a liquidiser, purée the pine kernels, garlic and shallot with the reserved asparagus cooking water.

Feed in the parsley, little by little, with the liquidiser going all the time.

Pour in the olive oil. You should have a vivid green dipping sauce. Add the lemon juice, salt and pepper, a little at a time until you are happy with the balance of the parsley pesto sauce.

INGREDIENTS

6 asparagus spears
1 tablespoon pine kernels
1 small clove garlic
1 shallot or 2 spring onions
50 g (2 oz) flat parsley, washed
120 ml (4 fl oz) olive oil
Juice of 1 lemon
Salt and pepper

MOROCCAN SWEET AND SOUR LEEKS

S E R V E S

—— 4 ——

1 kg (2 lb) leeks
2 cloves of garlic, crushed
1 tablespoon soft brown
sugar
60 ml (2¼ fl oz) olive oil
Juice of 1 lemon

These may be served hot as an appetiser as well as cold on a salad.

Wash and trim the leeks (see page 83). You really want only the white parts although a little green will do no harm providing it is tender.

Cut the leeks in half lengthwise. If the leeks are particularly long then cut each half into 5 cm (2 inch) pieces. Dry thoroughly.

In a large pan or frying-pan fry the garlic and sugar in the olive oil until the colour starts to turn brown. Stir constantly.

Add the leeks and cook them over a moderate heat until they take on colour from the caramelising sugar and oil. Pour on the lemon juice and stir.

Cover the pan with a lid and cook gently until tender, about 15 minutes. If you prefer you can cook these in a low oven (Gas Mark 3, 160°C, 325°F) in a roasting tray covered with foil.

Grated carrot salad with cinnamon, lemon and honey

SERVES

— 4 —

This is a dish for good quality carrots, organically grown perhaps. At any rate avoid woody specimens or the tasteless Dutch baby variety.

Whisk the olive oil, lemon juice, honey and cinnamon together.

Toss the carrot and sultanas in the dressing. Season with salt and pepper to taste.

INGREDIENTS

85 ml (3 fl oz) olive oil
Juice of 1 lemon
1 tablespoon honey
1 teaspoon ground cinnamon
450 g (1 lb) carrots, peeled and grated
50 g (2 oz) sultanas
Salt and pepper

BITTER SALADS WITH WARM ASPARAGUS AND SESAME DRESSING

SERVES

—— 4 ——

INGREDIENTS

FOR THE SALAD

16 asparagus spears

A selection of salad leaves
  from curly endive, lollo
  rosso, oakleaf lettuce,
  batavia, Belgian chicory,
  corn salad

1 avocado

15 g (½ oz) pine kernels

FOR THE DRESSING

3 tablespoons light sesame
  oil

7.5 g (¼ oz) pine kernels

1 sprig of fresh coriander

1 small knob of ginger,
  peeled and finely
  chopped

1 teaspoon soy sauce

A few drops of lemon juice

1 tablespoon water

Bitter lettuces like frizzy endive, Belgian chicory and radicchio used to be winter salads only. Now that they are available year round they can be paired with English asparagus when it is in season and at its cheapest in May.

Boil the asparagus for 5 to 10 minutes, depending on how thick they are. They should still be fairly crunchy.

Toast the pine kernels on a baking tray under a hot grill until golden brown.

Make a salad with the lettuces, avocado and pine kernels and dress it initially with a tablespoon of the light sesame oil. If you can only find dark sesame oil mix it, half and half, with groundnut or vegetable oil or it will be too strong.

Combine all the other dressing ingredients in a liquidiser. It should produce a creamy, sauce-like dressing.

Place the warm asparagus in the salad and spoon some dressing on to each plate to serve.

SIDE DISHES

Side dishes represent vegetables' traditional role in the dinnertime scheme of things. However they should not be merely an afterthought. People faced with endless permutations of peas, carrots and sprouts at the table will become very bored. Quite rightly.

In my restaurant, the vegetable component of each main course is of major importance, regularly doubling as sauce or relish to whatever it accompanies.

A word of caution though. Once you move away from simple treatments like boiling or steaming and start adding herbs, oil or cream you inevitably reduce the vegetable's suitability as an all-purpose accompaniment. A stir-fry will not taste as good if served on the same plate as anything creamy, the soy sauce reacts with dairy products to give a very salty taste. Similarly, Spiced Red Cabbage (page 108) and Grated Marrow with Dill (page 101) are both robust though tasty treatments so think about their effect on whatever else shares the plate.

Of course, having given it some thought, you may conclude that you will carry on with the stir-fry or grated marrow and change the rest.

A meal is made interesting by contrasts. Not just contrasts of colour but also of temperature, texture and seasoning. If you are planning a stew or pot roast, aim for something firm to go with it, perhaps Couscous (page 72) or even just crisp French bread. Grilled or roast food will marry well with something soft like Basil and Olive Oil Mashed Potato (page 111) or a vegetable in a sauce like the baby Turnips with Mustard (page 98). A good salad tossed in a sharp dressing will give a change of pace to the meal and doesn't involve too much time or trouble.

The important thing is to have thought about your combination. If, having thought, you decide on carrots and peas, that is fine. If having thought, you come up with carrots and peas every day, it could be time for the doctor to take a look at your thinking processes.

CONTENTS

PEPPER AND SWEETCORN PUDDING

SERVES
—— 4 ——

Preheat the oven to Gas Mark 4, 180°C (350°F).

Cut the pepper into chunks. Process briefly in a food processor then add the corn.

Process for a few seconds so that the sweetcorn kernels are broken but are not puréed.

Mix in the cream and season with salt and pepper.

Butter an ovenproof dish and pour in the mixture. Dot any remaining butter on top then bake in the oven for 30 minutes or until the top is golden brown.

INGREDIENTS

1 large red pepper, halved and de-seeded
450 g (1 lb) sweetcorn, tinned, frozen or scraped from the cob
300 ml (10 fl oz) double cream
Salt and pepper
50 g (2 oz) butter

TURNIPS WITH MUSTARD

SERVES

—— 4 ——

INGREDIENTS

450 g (1 lb) baby turnips
150 ml (5 fl oz) double
  cream or (better) crème
  fraîche
1 tablespoon coarse-grain
  mustard
A few drops of lemon juice
Salt and pepper

Generally turnips are coarse, dull vegetables well suited to their poor reputation. Baby turnips, often sold in bunches with their leaves intact, are on the other hand well worth using. They are not fibrous like their older relatives and will cook quite quickly.

Peel the turnips. As with all vegetables which are to be cooked together, try to select specimens of roughly equal size so that they cook evenly.

Boil in salted water for 10 minutes then drain and season. Leave to one side while you make the sauce.

Bring the cream, mustard and lemon juice to the boil then add the turnips. Boil the vegetables for a few seconds in the sauce, stirring continuously, so that they are coated. Season to taste and serve.

CREAMED LEEKS

S E R V E S
— 4 —

Any fresh herb such as tarragon or basil will add an extra dimension to this side dish. It will also make the flavour of the creamed leeks a more dominant part of the meal so you will need to give thought to the overall balance of the other flavours on your plate and check whether the herbs will complement or conflict with them.

Wash and prepare the leeks (see page 83). Simmer in boiling, salted water until tender. The time this takes will vary with the age and thickness of the leeks. Tender new-season leeks will cook in less than 10 minutes, coarse thick ones could take twice as long. Drain.

Melt the butter over low heat. Don't let it go brown.

Add the flour and stir into a soft roux. Let it cook over the low heat for 1 minute before adding the milk, little by little. Stir until this comes back to the boil. It will look like a thick white porridge.

Add the cream, mustard and a scant teaspoonful of salt and bring to the boil, stirring all the time.

Add the poached leeks to the saucepan and carefully mix them with the cream sauce. The leeks will almost certainly have retained some of their cooking water which will thin down the sauce but should it still be too thick add a little more milk.

Depending on what the leeks are to accompany you could add some grated nutmeg, chopped herbs or grated cheese to serve.

INGREDIENTS

8 medium leeks
50 g (2 oz) butter
25 g (1 oz) plain flour
300 ml (10 fl oz) milk
150 ml (5 fl oz) single
  cream
1 tablespoon Dijon mustard
Salt
Nutmeg, herbs, grated
  cheese, to serve
  (optional)

BRUSSELS SPROUTS WITH LEMON AND BUTTERED BREADCRUMBS

SERVES
— 4 —

INGREDIENTS

450 g (1 lb) button
  Brussels sprouts
6 tablespoons breadcrumbs
  (see page 17)
50 g (2 oz) butter
Juice of ½ lemon
Salt and pepper

Prepare the sprouts by cutting off the stem ends and any wilted or discoloured outer leaves. Leave the sprouts in cold salted water for 5 minutes.

Boil the sprouts for 6 to 10 minutes in salted water. They should be tender but not soft. Drain well.

Fry the breadcrumbs in the butter until brown. Add the sprouts and season with salt and pepper. Squeeze the lemon juice over and serve.

GRATED MARROW WITH DILL AND SOURED CREAM

S E R V E S
—— 4 ——

Cut the marrow into matchstick-sized threads. If you have a vegetable mandoline or food processor attachment which will do the job, so much the better.

Sprinkle the marrow with a teaspoon of salt and leave it for 30 minutes. Squeeze out the brine which forms.

Fry the onion in the vegetable oil until soft. Add 120 ml (4 fl oz) of water, then the marrow. Bring to the boil.

Mix the soured cream and flour together to a thin paste then pour it into the pan. Bring to the boil, stirring all the time.

Add the dill and let the resulting mix simmer for a few minutes. Finish the dish with some milled black pepper and a few drops of vinegar.

INGREDIENTS

1.5 kg (3 lb) vegetable marrow or courgettes, peeled
Salt
1 small onion, peeled and chopped
50 ml (2 fl oz) vegetable oil
300 ml (10 fl oz) soured cream
25 g (1 oz) plain flour
1 small bunch of dill, chopped
Black pepper
A few drops of malt or wine vinegar

GRATIN DE JABRON

SERVES

—— 4 ——

1 kg (2 lb) maincrop
  potatoes
175 g (6 oz) butter
3 cloves garlic, peeled and
  crushed
Salt and freshly ground
  black pepper
300 ml (10 fl oz) milk
300 ml (10 fl oz) double
  cream

This is my favourite version of *gratin dauphinoise* potatoes. Also it is the least difficult.

Preheat the oven to Gas Mark 4, 180°C (350°F).

Try to select potatoes of an approximately equal size.
You are going to boil them in their skins so if they have
been graded they will cook more evenly. Give them a
good wash.

Boil the potatoes until they are just cooked, about
12–15 minutes. If the potatoes are a floury variety and
overcooked they will be difficult to handle. Drain off the
water then peel the skins.

Cut the potatoes into 5 mm (¼ inch) slices.

Melt the butter and garlic together in a frying-pan.
When the butter is hot – but before it starts to colour –
add the potato slices and turn them over so that they are
coated with the butter and garlic mixture. Unless you
have a particularly large frying-pan you will probably
need to do this in two or three batches. Season the
potatoes with salt and pepper. This stage can be done
anything up to a day in advance and the tossed potato
kept covered in the fridge, if it suits you better.

Spread the potato on to a shallow greased ovenproof
dish. Pour on the milk and cream and bake, uncovered,
for 20 minutes until the top is golden brown.

PEPPER AND SWEETCORN PUDDING (*page 97*)

CHAMP

S E R V E S

—— 4 ——

This dish was one of my favourite childhood lunches. I have heard of champ being made with leeks, cabbage and other greens much in the same way as Colcannon or Bubble and Squeak but if you have good potatoes there is no better variation than this.

This is pure comfort food. Don't be tempted to skimp on butter or milk. Obsessive slimmers should turn to another page.

INGREDIENTS

750 g (1½ lb) maincrop potatoes, peeled
10 spring onions
300 ml (10 fl oz) milk
Salt and pepper
100 g (4 oz) – at least – salted butter

Boil the potatoes until done, about 15 minutes.

Meanwhile, chop the white part of the spring onions and poach them in the milk for 10 minutes. Chop the green part of the spring onions and keep them to one side.

Drain the potatoes and mash them. Season with salt and pepper to taste. Beat in the warm milk and white onion mixture.

Put a mound of potato on each plate and press a well into the centre of each.

Put a large knob of salted butter and the chopped green parts of the spring onion into the well in each mound.

BANANA AND CARAMEL PANCAKES (*page 118*)

MANGE-TOUT PEAS

SERVES

—— 4 ——

INGREDIENTS

450 g (1 lb) mange-tout
  peas
50 g (2 oz) butter
1 tablespoon chopped fresh
  herbs of your choice
Lemon juice
Salt and pepper

Fresh peas, the usual kind, are only worth considering if you happen to live close by where they are grown or grow them yourself. Kept any length of time, they harden like bullets and only suit braising or soup making.

Mange-touts have filled the mealtime gap for people bored with frozen peas. They have some of the sweet freshness of garden peas albeit with a different texture. For most of the year the varieties on offer are larger than ideal and this treatment works well with them. During the few weeks that tiny Jersey ones are available you won't even need to slice them.

———

Top and tail the mange-tout pods, pulling away any string.

Slice each lengthwise into three so that you have matchstick-sized strips.

Drop these into boiling, salted water. They are cooked as soon as the water reboils.

Lift them out with a slotted spoon. Pour off almost all the water, leaving about 150 ml (5 fl oz).

Stir in the butter and boil hard for 1 minute so that it emulsifies. Add the herbs, a squeeze of lemon juice and season with salt and pepper. Return the mange-touts to the pan. Turn them with the herb butter and serve.

Don't ever toss mange-touts in only butter for they quickly become greasy and unappetising.

ULSTER POTATO BREAD

S E R V E S

—— 4 ——

Not really bread at all, these potato cakes are often served as part of a breakfast fry-up in Northern Ireland. They are also fine served with cheese or salad and will keep for a couple of days without ill-effect. Cook the potatoes in advance.

——————

Cut the potatoes into approximately equal sized pieces. Boil them in salted water until tender, about 15 minutes. Drain and mash them. Salt the potato well and stir in the knob of butter. Allow to cool.

Turn the mashed potato out on to a floured work-surface. You will need to incorporate about a third of its volume of plain flour. As you work in the flour, the dough becomes easier to handle.

Roll out the dough to 8 mm (⅓ inch) thickness. Dust with a little flour and cut into triangles or whatever shape you fancy.

Griddle the potato bread on a dry frying-pan over a moderate to low heat for about 3 minutes on each side. Keep them in an airtight container until needed.

INGREDIENTS

450 g (1 lb) maincrop potatoes, peeled
Salt
15 g (½ oz) butter
100 g (4 oz) plain flour

SPICED RED CABBAGE

SERVES

—— 4 ——

*1 small to medium red
cabbage
1 onion, peeled and sliced
A little vegetable oil
120 ml (4 fl oz) red wine
120 ml (4 fl oz) orange
juice
Salt, pepper, ground
cinnamon and nutmeg*

Red cabbage will temporarily discolour your fingers as you are chopping it. If this is a problem wear rubber gloves. Cut the cabbage into quarters and cut out the hard white core.

Shred the cabbage. Either cut it into strips or use an attachment in a food processor.

Use a heavy-based saucepan if you have one. Fry the onion in a little oil for 2 minutes then add the shredded red cabbage.

Pour on the red wine and orange juice. Season with plenty (a teaspoon of each) of cinnamon, nutmeg, salt and pepper. Cover the pan with a tight-fitting lid and when the pot comes to the boil turn down the heat to a steady simmer.

Cook gently for around 15 minutes or until done. The cabbage will cook fairly rapidly because of the steam created by the evaporating wine and orange juice. Stir the cabbage occasionally to make sure it doesn't stick to the bottom of the pan.

SPINACH

SERVES
—— 4 ——

As a child it took more than Popeye to make me eat spinach. Now it is among my favourites. Frozen spinach bears most of the blame, it is an awful product and no substitute for the genuine article. Unless you intend puréeing the stuff you will find too much stalk and a substandard texture. It is in any case quicker to pick over, wash, and cook fresh spinach than wait for frozen to thaw so there you have it, spinach comes from the greengrocer not the freezer centre.

Unscrupulous greengrocers could sell you spinach beet as spinach. However this is a tough winter substitute. You can always tell what is good by assessing it as potential salad. If it looks and feels tender enough to eat raw it will cook beautifully, if not buy cabbage instead.

Pick over the leaves and discard any yellow or brown ones.

Tear off any particularly thick stalks.

Wash in enough water to suspend the spinach and dunk the leaves down to loosen any sand or grit. Spinach picked after rain can be quite gritty.

Take your widest saucepan – a wok is good – and bring 5 mm (¼ inch) depth of salted water to the boil. Drop in the spinach and turn the leaves over as they wilt in the heat. Cover and boil hard for 3 or 4 minutes or until all the spinach is soft.

Turn it out into a colander and press with a fish slice to get rid of excess water. You will have about half the weight of spinach than you had when you started and even less volume.

My own preference is to finish the spinach with nutmeg, pepper and a large knob of butter. Pistachio nuts or flaked almonds are also fine provided they do not conflict with anything else on the plate.

INGREDIENTS

1 kg (2 lb) raw spinach
Nutmeg, pepper, butter,
  pistachio nuts or
  almonds, to serve
  (all optional)

CELERIAC
AND POTATO PURÉE

SERVES

— 4 —

INGREDIENTS

*450 g (1 lb) floury
maincrop potatoes,
peeled*
*450 g (1 lb) celeriac,
peeled*
50 g (2 oz) butter
*65 ml (2½ fl oz) double
cream*
65 ml (2½ fl oz) milk
Salt and pepper

Cut the potatoes into approximately equal sized pieces and boil in salted water until cooked, about 15 minutes. Drain and purée either with a masher or by pushing through a sieve.

Cut the celeriac into 5 mm (¼ inch) cubes. Boil in salted water until soft, around 7 minutes. Drain then purée in the same way as the potatoes.

Add the butter, cream and milk to the mashed potato.

Beat in the celeriac purée and season with salt and pepper to taste.

BASIL AND OLIVE OIL MASHED POTATO

SERVES
— 4 —

Good served with grilled vegetables as a textural contrast. The potato should be soft, a sauce as well as a vegetable.

—————

Cut the potatoes into approximately equal pieces and boil in salted water until cooked, around 15 minutes. Drain well.

Either push the potatoes through a sieve or mash with a potato masher. In either case you don't want lumps so mash well and don't add any liquid.

Season with nutmeg, salt and pepper.

Liquidise the basil and olive oil together in a blender. Some blenders don't function well with small quantities. If you find this a problem add some – or all – of the cream.

Stir the cream into the mashed potato over a low heat. Finally, add the basil and olive oil mixture and beat hard for a few seconds to fluff up the potato.

INGREDIENTS

450 g (1 lb) maincrop
   potatoes, peeled
1 large bunch of fresh basil
50 ml (2 fl oz) olive oil
120 ml (4 fl oz) double
   cream
Nutmeg, salt and pepper

BROCCOLI STALKS
STIR-FRY

SERVES
—— 4 ——

There are times of year when broccoli seems to be 90 per cent stalk. Strangely, this can be the best time to buy them as the stalks, properly handled, are much more of a treat than the florets.

They need to be prepared like this.

Cut off any florets. You can use these in the dish also or save them for another time.

Use a sharp knife to peel away the outer layer of each stem. You can tell when you reach the right depth as the colour and texture of the stalk lightens.

You will be left with a crisp, crunchy, asparagus-like vegetable totally different in texture to the peel. If these stalks are thick cut them into slices, otherwise cut them into roughly equal lengths.

Once prepared, broccoli stalks can be eaten raw like celery. If they are to be cooked then it should be lightly as they are delicate and will cook quickly.

———

Heat a wok or frying-pan. Add the oil.

Add the broccoli and cook for 2 minutes.

Add the soy sauce, water and chilli sauce and cook for a further 2 minutes. Serve immediately.

INGREDIENTS

1 tablespoon groundnut or
   light sesame oil
1 kg (2 lb) broccoli
1 tablespoon Japanese soy
   sauce or oyster sauce
1 tablespoon water
A dash of chilli sauce

BROAD BEANS WITH CREAM AND SAVORY

SERVES

— 4 —

Removing broad beans from their pods is a swift task, although it is disappointing to see how little you end up with to eat from comparatively large quantities of broad beans. Old or large specimens also need the white casing removed from each bean, a tiresome process. This treatment will deal with shopping's realities, that you will have a proportion of both large and small.

Summer savory is a powerful herb that goes well with broad beans but not much else. Use sage if you can't find any.

————

Fry the onion gently in the butter until soft.

Add the water. Bring to the boil then add the beans. Cover and boil for 5 minutes or until tender.

Lift out around half the beans with a slotted spoon. Pick out the smallest and most tender if you can. Alternatively peel off the white skins of the large ones you have scooped out. Keep these to one side.

Add the cream, a little salt, sugar and pepper to the pan and then purée in a liquidiser or rub through a sieve.

Reboil, adding the chopped herbs. Stir in the beans you picked out earlier and serve.

INGREDIENTS

1 small onion, chopped
50 g (2 oz) butter
600 ml (1 pint) water
450 g (1 lb) shelled weight
    of broad beans,
    approximately 1.5 kg
    (3 lb) unshelled weight
65 ml (2½ fl oz) single
    cream
Salt, pepper and sugar
1 teaspoon chopped fresh
    savory

CARAMELISED SHALLOTS

SERVES

— 4 —

225 g (8 oz) shallots
25 g (1 oz) butter
1 tablespoon granulated
* sugar*
Salt

Cooking shallots with sugar may seem a little bizarre but isn't. Sugar features in the recipes for classic dishes like French onion soup and partners members of the onion family surprisingly well.

If the main dish will stand it, a few rosemary leaves would go well with this.

Preheat the oven to Gas Mark 4, 180°C (350°F).

Peel the shallots. Don't worry if a little skin remains on the stalks of the shallots.

Fry them in the butter over a high heat so that they become a little brown.

Add the sugar. Carry on frying until the sugar turns brown and coats the shallots. Shake the pan frequently.

Transfer the shallots into a greased ovenproof dish and season with salt. Bake for 15 to 20 minutes until they are dark brown, soft and slightly sticky.

The frying-pan and ovenproof dish will look a nightmare to clean but are in fact very easy. Sugar, even caramelised sugar, will dissolve completely in water given a few minutes' soaking.

PUDDINGS

'No afters unless you eat all your greens.' Most children will have been on the receiving end of this familiar threat at some point, and nowhere is it more appropriate than at the end of a vegetable recipe book.

Someone once told me that rhubarb is a vegetable not a fruit. This is the sort of irrelevance which need not concern us here. Tomatoes are fruit but we don't want them in our fruit salad. More disturbing is the trend for fruit to make a gratuitous appearance in the salads and garnishes of many pub and restaurant meals.

It is very gross to have chunks of unpeeled kiwifruit or orange lurking in one's salad and I wonder who is responsible for popularising the habit. Fruit is acceptable with rich or gamey meat, it is supposed to cut through excess fattiness and to complement the taste of well-hung game. The acidity of lemon or lime juice will lift an otherwise bland or dull dish in the same way as a dash of vinegar. But bananas, melons and grapes need to be used with great care.

The ideal place for your fruit is here at the end of the meal where the sweetness and freshness will make a fine reward for having eaten all your vegetables.

The following recipes are reasonably easy. The Raspberry Tart (page 117) needs some care but not necessarily great skill or time. If the oven is too hot the custard in which the raspberries cook will curdle or soufflé up. Otherwise you have no worries.

CONTENTS

RASPBERRY TART

SERVES

—— 4 ——

Make the sweet pastry ahead of time or else buy ready-made. Don't hurry the baking process along by raising the oven temperature or you will have a sweet scrambled egg dish instead.

If this recipe is only on the fringe of being 'quick and easy', it is worth the extra minutes for the results.

Preheat the oven to Gas Mark 8, 230°C (450°F).

Make the sweet pastry. Whisk the butter and egg together. Add the sugar and salt. Lastly, stir in the flour. Knead it two or three times just to ensure everything is well mixed. Refrigerate for at least 30 minutes or until needed.

Roll out the pastry and line a buttered or non–stick 25 cm (10 in) tart case with it. Bake it blind for 10 minutes in the oven.

Make the filling. Whisk the egg, egg yolks and sugar together with the cream.

Place the raspberries in the tart and pour the egg and cream mixture over them.

Reduce the oven temperature to Gas Mark 4, 180°C (350°F) and bake until set, about 40 minutes. Take care not to have the oven hotter than this or the custard may curdle. Equally good served hot, warm or cold.

INGREDIENTS

FOR THE SWEET PASTRY
150 g (5 oz) butter,
  softened
1 egg
50 g (2 oz) caster sugar
A pinch of salt
225 g (8 oz) plain flour

FOR THE FILLING
1 whole egg
2 egg yolks
65 g (2½ oz) caster sugar
150 ml (5 fl oz) double
  cream
1 punnet of raspberries,
  approximately 100 g
  (4 oz)

BANANA AND CARAMEL PANCAKES

SERVES

— 4 —

FOR THE PANCAKE BATTER

100 g (4 oz) plain flour
175 ml (6 fl oz) milk
50 ml (2 fl oz) water
A pinch of salt
1 teaspoon sugar
2 eggs
25 g (1 oz) butter, melted
Vegetable oil for frying

FOR THE CARAMEL SAUCE

25 g (1 oz) butter
50 g (2 oz) brown sugar
1 tablespoon golden syrup
150 ml (5 fl oz) double cream

4 bananas, peeled
Icing sugar, to serve

For reasons I can't fully explain, the taste of caramel and butterscotch seems particularly British. Maybe it's something to do with all the boiled sweets we eat as children.

Be careful when making caramel that you don't burn yourself. Sugar caramelises (turns brown) at quite a high temperature, by which time all the water will have evaporated away. When the sugar starts to colour, remove the saucepan from direct heat, let the sugar syrup subside for a second, then add a few drops of water to arrest the cooking process. It will handle easily from then on.

Don't become alarmed if the pan looks as if it will take for ever to clean. In fact, unless you really have burnt it, all it needs is contact with water for half an hour or so. Sugar naturally forms syrup and will blend with another liquid fairly quickly. Confectioners and pastrycooks who make fruit baskets, flowers and the like from pulled sugar keep their masterpieces in airtight display cases to prevent the sugar combining with moisture in the air and disintegrating.

Preheat the oven to Gas Mark 5, 190°C (375°F).

Make the pancake batter by whisking together all the batter ingredients. Fry the pancakes in the vegetable oil and keep warm while you make the sauce.

Make the caramel sauce by melting the butter and adding the sugar. Stir until the sugar dissolves and then boil until it starts to colour. This will take about 5 minutes. Then add the syrup and cream and bring back to the boil.

Slice the bananas and heat them through in the caramel sauce.

Place each pancake over a greased ramekin dish or small ovenproof container then spoon some of the banana and caramel mixture into each one.

Lift the corners of each pancake up and tuck over into the edges of the ramekin dishes so that the filling is completely wrapped in pancake.

Put the pancakes into the oven to reheat for 5 minutes then turn out on to warmed plates and dust with icing sugar to serve.

CLAFOUTIS

SERVES

—— 4 ——

INGREDIENTS

4 eggs
100 g (4 oz) caster sugar
A pinch of salt
100 g (4 oz) plain flour
450 ml (15 fl oz) milk
½ teaspoon vanilla essence
50 g (2 oz) butter
400 g (14 oz) stoned
  cherries
Icing sugar, to serve

This is an upmarket cherries in batter which originates from the Limousin area of France. A tablespoon of rum or brandy in the batter will add an extra dimension to it. A good-quality tin or jar of cherries would make a reasonable substitute for fresh cherries should there be none available.

Preheat the oven to Gas Mark 4, 180°C (350°F).

Beat the eggs, caster sugar and salt together.

Beat in the flour, add the milk and vanilla essence and mix until smooth.

Melt the butter. Use half to grease the baking dish (use an ovenproof dish rather than a metal baking dish). Add the remaining butter to the batter.

Scatter the cherries in the baking dish and pour over the batter.

Bake in the oven until cooked, around 40 minutes. You can test it by piercing with a knife or skewer and seeing whether the batter still clings to it. Dust with icing sugar to serve.

WARM PEARS WITH BUTTERSCOTCH

SERVES

— 4 —

To make the sauce, melt the butter and sugar together in a heavy-based pan and cook until dark brown. Lift the saucepan off the heat then add the syrup and cream. Reboil and keep warm while you prepare the pears.

Slice the pears in half lengthwise and take out the core. Slice the pears like fans and put under a hot grill until the pears warm and some of their natural sugars caramelise. Serve with the sauce.

INGREDIENTS

FOR THE SAUCE
50 g (2 oz) butter
100 g (4 oz) demerara
  sugar
2 tablespoons golden syrup
300 ml (10 fl oz) double
  cream

4 pears, Williams or
  Comice, peeled

121

WARM COMPOTE OF RHUBARB, STRAWBERRIES AND GINGER

SERVES
— 4 —

INGREDIENTS

450 g (1 lb) rhubarb
100 g (4 oz) granulated sugar
50 g (2 oz) stem ginger, finely diced
1 punnet strawberries (approximately 225 g/ 8 oz)
Clotted cream or vanilla ice-cream, to serve

Cut the rhubarb into 2.5 cm (1 inch) lengths.

Place in a saucepan with the sugar and stem ginger. Cover and boil for 5 minutes until the sugar caramelises.

Cut the strawberries into halves or quarters according to size. Taste the syrup produced from boiling the rhubarb and sugar. Add more sugar if necessary then stir in the strawberries. Serve warm with clotted cream or vanilla ice-cream.

APPLE TARTS

SERVES
— 4 —

Preheat the oven to Gas Mark 8, 230°C (450°F).

Roll out the pastry 3 mm (⅛ inch) thick.

Cut four rounds about 18 cm (7 inches) in diameter. Place on a greased baking tray.

Peel and core the apples. Cut them in half then slice each half thinly. Arrange the slices, neatly overlapping, on the pastry rounds.

Mix the sugar with the cinnamon then sprinkle it over the apple tarts.

Cut the butter into small dice and dot this over the tarts.

Bake in the oven for 25 minutes.

Meanwhile warm the jam with a tablespoon of water and when the tarts are cooked brush them with this glaze. Serve with clotted cream or vanilla ice-cream.

INGREDIENTS

450 g (1 lb) puff pastry
2 eating apples, Granny
  Smiths for preference
65 g (2½ oz) granulated
  sugar
½ teaspoon ground
  cinnamon
50 g (2 oz) unsalted butter
4 tablespoons apricot jam
Clotted cream or vanilla
  ice-cream, to serve

123

GOOSEBERRY FOOL WITH BRANDYSNAPS

SERVES

— 4 —

FOR THE FOOL

450 g (1 lb) fresh
gooseberries
175 g (6 oz) caster sugar
300 ml (10 fl oz) double
cream

FOR THE BRANDYSNAPS

100 g (4 oz) granulated
sugar
100 g (4 oz) butter
100 g (4 oz) golden syrup
100 g (4 oz) plain flour
10 g (¼ oz) ground ginger
Juice of ½ lemon
1 tablespoon brandy

Fools were originally fruit custards made with egg yolks and lots of spices. Nowadays they are made only with sieved fruit, sugar and cream or milk and generally served in a glass like syllabub. The brandysnap biscuits act as container as well as providing a contrast of texture in this version.

Preheat the oven to Gas Mark 4, 180°C (350°F).

Make the brandysnaps. Melt the sugar, butter and syrup together.

Warm the flour and add this and the ginger, lemon juice and brandy, mix together. Don't whisk or beat for any length of time, it doesn't matter if the mixture isn't completely smooth.

Spoon the mixture at 15 cm (6 in) intervals on to an oiled baking tray, or better still on to baking parchment or a non-stick surface and bake in the oven for 10 minutes until brown. The mixture will make 4 large brandysnaps.

As they start to cool, lift the biscuits with a palette knife or egg slice on to upturned cups or sugar bowls. When cool they will then be set into shapes usable as containers for your gooseberry fool. Leave to set.

Make the fool. Wash, top and tail the gooseberries. Place in a pan without water over moderate heat. Cover and then simmer the fruit for about 15 minutes. It will produce plenty of liquid.

Pour the gooseberries and their liquid into a blender, add the sugar then purée until smooth. Divide the purée into two equal parts and allow to cool.

Whip the cream then fold into one-half of the purée. Chill in the coldest part of the refrigerator for at least 10 minutes, longer if you have time.

To serve, combine the two gooseberry mixtures slightly so that you have a ripple effect of the purée and the creamy fool. Spoon into the brandysnap baskets.

Brandysnaps are easy but not foolproof. I once had an embarrassing experience when demonstrating a dish using them. An assistant had weighed out all the ingredients carefully but when adding the syrup had left a fair amount still coating the bowl in which it had been stored. The biscuits disintegrated on contact with the upturned sugar bowls. All very humiliating with fifty persons watching. I'm sure you would be more careful.

PEACHES IN RASPBERRY SAUCE

S E R V E S

— 4 —

4 large ripe peaches
100 g (4 oz) granulated
*   sugar*
1 tablespoon lemon juice

FOR THE SAUCE

2 punnets raspberries, each
*   approximately 100 g*
*   (4 oz)*
1 tablespoon lemon juice
1 tablespoon icing sugar

One of the great combinations, peaches and raspberries are in peak condition and at their cheapest simultaneously.

Pour boiling water over the peaches to loosen the skins then peel carefully.

Mix the sugar, lemon juice and 150 ml (5 fl oz) of the boiling water to make a syrup.

Put the peaches into the syrup, turning them so that they are coated.

Make the sauce by puréeing the raspberries, lemon juice and icing sugar in a liquidiser.

Put a peach in each serving dish and coat with raspberry sauce. Decorate with whipped cream or ice-cream if you wish.

ELIZABETH MOXON'S LEMON POSSET

SERVES

—— 4 ——

This was a regular dessert at Robert Carrier's restaurant in Islington, London. It looks similar to a syllabub but is much lighter and fresher tasting.

Grate the rind of both lemons into a bowl then squeeze the lemon juice on top. Stir in the sugar and wine.

Whisk the egg white until stiff.

Whisk the cream. As it begins to stiffen trickle in the wine, lemon juice and sugar mixture. Continue whisking until stiff.

Fold in the whisked egg white and then spoon or pipe into glasses to serve. This will keep, refrigerated, for up to a day. If it collapses you can rescue it by rewhipping it but it will lose its volume.

INGREDIENTS

2 lemons
50 g (2 oz) caster sugar
150 ml (5 fl oz) dry white wine
2 egg whites
600 ml (1 pint) double cream

RED FRUIT SALAD WITH CINNAMON ICE-CREAM

SERVES

— 4 —

FOR THE FRUIT SALAD

225 g (8 oz) cherries, pitted

1 punnet ripe raspberries, approximately 100 g (4 oz)

1 punnet ripe strawberries, approximately 225 g (8 oz)

1 punnet ripe tayberries approximately 100 g (4 oz)

½ punnet redcurrants approximately 50 g (2 oz)

75 g (3 oz) caster sugar

Juice of 1 lemon

150 ml (5 fl oz) water

1 tablespoon cognac

FOR THE ICE-CREAM

8 egg yolks

75 g (3 oz) caster sugar

300 ml (10 fl oz) milk

300 ml (10 fl oz) double cream

1 teaspoon ground cinnamon, or 2 sticks of cinnamon, to decorate

This is my 'desert island' pudding. It's only practical to make it in the summer with sun-ripened soft fruit in the peak of condition, and is related in concept to summer pudding – just simpler and better.

It's only worth making the cinnamon ice-cream if you have a sorbet machine. Otherwise buy a top-quality vanilla ice-cream and crumble some cinnamon sticks on top.

Make the ice-cream a little in advance. Whisk the egg yolks and sugar together then boil the milk and cream together and combine the two mixtures. Stir the custard over a low heat until the texture thickens slightly, showing it has cooked. Leave the custard to cool then churn in a sorbet or ice-cream machine.

Make the fruit salad. Start by cleaning all the fruit thoroughly.

Bring the cherries, sugar, lemon juice and water to the boil then allow to cool.

Add the cognac and all the other fruit. Leave to macerate for 10 minutes while you remove the ice-cream from the freezer and allow it to soften.

Make and churn the ice-cream as near as possible to when you intend eating it. Superficially it may seem that frozen desserts of any sort can be prepared well in advance. In fact home-made ice-cream shouldn't be kept any longer in the freezer than you would keep the custard in a fridge. Remember that commercial companies add preservatives and are geared up to thorough pasteurisation.

WARM CHOCOLATE CAKE WITH CHERRY COMPOTE

SERVES

— 4 —

The chocolate cake is of course also good served cold with tea or coffee. Cakes with little or no flour suffer if overcooked so try to avoid this pitfall. Even if the centre is a little underdone it will just taste soft and chocolatey rather than raw.

———

Preheat the oven to Gas Mark 4, 180°C (350°F).

Make the chocolate cake. Melt the chocolate pieces and butter together. This must be done gently, the best way being to put the chocolate and butter into a bowl and stand the bowl in warm water, stirring occasionally.

Whisk the egg whites until stiff. Make sure to use a clean, dry bowl and whisk.

Separately whisk the yolks, icing sugar and vanilla essence together then add the cornflour. Whisk for a further minute or until the colour becomes perceptibly lighter.

Add the melted chocolate and butter and mix thoroughly. Next add the whisked egg white folding it in one-third at a time.

Line an 18 cm (7 in) cake tin with baking parchment and pour in the cake batter. Bake in the centre of the oven for 30 to 40 minutes until done.

Meanwhile, make the compote. Bring the water, sugar and lemon juice to the boil, stirring occasionally. Add the cherries and cover with a lid. Reboil and simmer for 5 minutes.

Serve a slice of chocolate cake with a spoonful of cherry compote and garnish with some toasted flaked almonds if you like.

INGREDIENTS

FOR THE CAKE

225 g (8 oz) plain chocolate, broken into pieces
100 g (4 oz) butter
4 eggs, separated into yolks and whites
225 g (8 oz) icing sugar
A few drops of vanilla essence
2 tablespoons cornflour

FOR THE COMPOTE

300 ml (10 fl oz) water
100 g (4 oz) granulated sugar
A few drops of lemon juice
225 g (8 oz) cherries
50 g (2 oz) flaked almonds, toasted, to serve (optional)

APPLE FRITTERS

SERVES

—— 4 ——

INGREDIENTS

FOR THE BATTER
50 g (2 oz) plain flour
A pinch of salt
65 ml (2½ fl oz) water
1 teaspoon melted butter
1 egg white

FOR THE APPLE
  MIXTURE
4 ripe apples, peeled
1 tablespoon caster sugar
A few drops of lemon juice
1 tablespoon rum

Vegetable oil for frying
*1 tablespoon ground
  cinnamon, to serve*
*1 tablespoon icing sugar,
  to serve*

To make the batter, whisk the flour, salt, water and butter together.

Using a clean whisk and a separate clean, dry bowl, whisk the egg white until stiff then fold it into the batter.

Cut the apples into small (5 mm/¼ inch) pieces and sprinkle them with the sugar, lemon juice and rum.

Mix in the batter and deep-fry, a spoonful of the apple and batter mixture at a time.

Mix the cinnamon and icing sugar together and sprinkle over the fritters to serve.

FOUR SEASONS' MENUS

These suggestions should suit both weather and market conditions.

SPRING:

Watercress and Potato Soup (see page 46)
Parsley and Spring Onion Tart in Walnut Pastry (see page 65)
Gooseberry Fool with Brandysnaps (see page 124)

SUMMER:

Tempura vegetables with summer salads (see page 26)
Courgette Risotto with Parmesan Cheese Sauce (see page 60)
Warm Chocolate Cake with Cherry Compôte (see page 129)

AUTUMN:

Caesar Salad (see page 89)
Caponata (Sicilian Vegetable Stew) (see page 76)
Apple Fritters (see page 130)

WINTER:

Mashed Potato Cakes with Olives and Capers (see page 23)
Filo Pastry Pie with Spinach and Goat's Cheese (see page 64)
Banana and Caramel Pancakes (see page 118)

INDEX

Page numbers in italics refer to illustrations

BBC BOOKS' QUICK AND EASY COOKERY

Launched in 1989 by Ken Hom and Sarah Brown, the *Quick and Easy Cookery* series is a culinary winner. Everything about the titles is aimed at quick and easy recipes – the store-cupboard introductions, the ingredients and cooking methods, the menu section at the back of the books. Eight pages of colour photographs are also included to provide a flash of inspiration for the frantic or faint-hearted.

Other titles in the series:

ALREADY PUBLISHED: *Beverley Piper's Quick and Easy Healthy Cookery*
Clare Connery's Quick and Easy Salads
Joanna Farrow's Quick and Easy Fish Cookery
Ken Hom's Quick and Easy Chinese Cookery
Sandeep Chatterjee's Quick and Easy Indian Vegetarian Cookery
Sarah Brown's Quick and Easy Vegetarian Cookery
Claire Macdonald's Quick and Easy Desserts and Puddings

TO COME:
Joanna Farrow's Quick and Easy Cake Decorating
Madhur Jaffrey's Quick and Easy Indian Cookery
Mary Berry's Quick and Easy Cakes
Linda Fraser's Quick and Easy Suppers

KEN HOM'S QUICK AND EASY CHINESE COOKERY

Ken Hom's best-selling *Chinese Cookery* has become the classic guide to the art of preparing Chinese food. Now, in his *Quick and Easy Chinese Cookery* he makes the most of traditional Chinese quick-cook techniques and shows you how to make mouth-watering and healthy meals in minutes.

JOANNA FARROW'S QUICK AND EASY FISH COOKERY

Is your idea of a quick and easy fish dish limited to fishfingers or fish and chips? If so, *Joanna Farrow's Quick and Easy Fish Cookery* will change all that. Joanna Farrow explodes the myth that cooking with fish is time-consuming and complicated. Her recipes are imaginative, simple to prepare and show how to get the best out of the exciting variety of fish now widely available.

CLARE CONNERY'S QUICK AND EASY SALADS

Imaginative salad recipes for all occasions, compiled in the popular 'quick and easy' format. Sunny Irish cook Clare Connery creates some delicious new salads, as well as spicing up some old favourites.

BEVERLEY PIPER'S QUICK AND EASY HEALTHY COOKERY

A fun, easy-to-read book designed for those who wish to follow a healthy diet but have limited time to cook. Each tasty recipe is accompanied by information about the nutritional value of the ingredients enabling you to cook really well-balanced meals.

SANDEEP CHATTERJEE'S QUICK AND EASY INDIAN VEGETARIAN COOKERY

Sandeep Chatterjee's Quick and Easy Indian Vegetarian Cookery is the first cookbook from Sandeep Chatterjee, the highly acclaimed chef from London's Bombay Brasserie. A wonderful introduction to Indian vegetarian food, with recipes which are quick and easy to make.

SARAH BROWN'S QUICK AND EASY VEGETARIAN COOKERY

Sarah Brown's recipes concentrate on main meals, with wholefood, vegetable and salad ingredients as their basis. There is also a chapter on soups and starters, a collection of recipes for delicious desserts and a selection of imaginative menus.

CLAIRE MACDONALD'S QUICK AND EASY DESSERTS AND PUDDINGS

Claire Macdonald provides 80 fabulous recipes for simple desserts and puddings. The recipes include traditional puddings such as pies, crumbles and custards as well as more sophisticated chocolate and fruit desserts.